Dr. Eugene L. Swearingen

Presented to:

_____

From:

_____

Date:

_____

Publisher's Note

A very special person once picked up this book – that person is you and that moment is now.

These "50 KEYS" will unlock the very best in you as you read them. Again and again.

Each time you visit these pages, you will be welcomed by Dr. Swearingen's sincerity and friendship. He has used these "50 KEYS" to achieve success in his life.

You can too.

Enjoy

CHAIR OF FREE ENTERPRISE
PUBLISHING HOUSE

SUCCESS
AND BEYOND

50 KEYS

by

Dr. Eugene L. Swearingen

Chair of Free Enterprise
Publishing House

2650 E. 66th
Tulsa, Oklahoma 74136
United States of America

Copyright © 1987 by Eugene L. Swearingen.
Revised 1996 by Eugene L. Swearingen.

All Rights reserved under International and Pan American Copyright Conventions.

ISBN 1-888798-90-4 Hardcover

No original part of this Work, including typesetting and layout, may be reproduced, used, or transmitted in any form or manner or by any means whatsoever, electronic or mechanical, including photocopying or recording, or by any information storage or retrieval system, except as may be expressly permitted by the 1976 Copyright Act or in writing from the Copyright holder.

First Hardcover Printing March 1996

Editing and Book Design: Kevin D. Decker and Keith T. Decker

10 9 8 7 6 5 4 3 2

Publisher's Cataloging-in-Publication Data
Swearingen, Dr. Eugene L.
  Success and Beyond: 50 Keys/Dr. Eugene L. Swearingen
  ISBN 1-888798-90-4 Hardcover
1. Success 2. Conduct of Life 3. Christian Life 4. Life Skills
5. Success in Business
158.1-dc20
Library of Congress Catalog Card Number: 96-83252

Printed in the U.S.A.

Dr. Eugene L. Swearingen

The key to why things change is the key to everything.
~ James Burke

DR. EUGENE L. SWEARINGEN

About the Author...

Dr. Eugene L. Swearingen, a former professor at Oral Roberts University, is the current Holder of the Chair of Free Enterprise. He received his Doctor of Philosophy in Economics from Stanford University.

He held all ranks from Instructor through Professor of Economics at Oklahoma State University. He was selected as Dean of the College of Business, and then Vice President of the University.

Dr. Swearingen became President of the University of Tulsa, then President of National Bank of Tulsa, which is now the Bank of Oklahoma. He was then promoted to Chairman of the Board and Chief Executive Officer.

As Editor of a case book on business policy now in its fourth Edition, Dr. Swearingen has published numerous articles. He has served extensively as a management consultant to business organizations and conducted Management Development Programs for many different companies. He is also past President of the National Council for Small Business Management Development.

Dr. Swearingen is listed in Who's Who in the World; Who's Who in American Education; Who's Who in Finance and Industry; Who's Who in America; Who's Who in Banking; Who's Who among Authors; and the Dictionary of International Biography.

He was inducted into the Oklahoma Hall of Fame, 1973, and into the Oklahoma State University Alumni Hall of Fame, 1978.

Having served as a Member of the Oklahoma State Regents for Higher Education, 1977-1986, Dr. Swearingen was Chairman and Member of the Board of

Trustees of the Southwestern Graduate School Foundation for Banking Education, 1977-1983.

Dr. Swearingen is past Chairman of the Executive Service Corps of Tulsa, and current Chairman of Local America Bank.

He loves mentoring young people on how to become successful.

DEDICATION

∞∞∞∞∞∞∞∞

This book is dedicated to the six men who have most influenced my life. Each one, in his own right, has contributed greatly to the welfare of Tulsa and Oklahoma.

Bob Parker, Sr.
A best friend for over thirty years. He was Chairman of the Selection Committee that selected me to be the President of the University of Tulsa.

John H. Williams
A super businessman who had faith that my managerial skills could be transferred to banking.

Bob Thomas
Entrepreneur and philanthropist, whose Gift founded the Chair of Free Enterprise which I hold at Oral Roberts University.

Jim Barnes
C.E.O. of Mapco, who supports the Chair of Free Enterprise and is the former student of mine of whom I am most proud.

Oral Roberts
Founder of O.R.U., who changed my career from banking back to education. He gave me the opportunity to remain young at heart by serving the fine young people of Oral Roberts University.

Wayne Swearingen
My brother and dear friend whom I value highly.

∞∞∞∞∞∞∞∞

Dr. Eugene L. Swearingen

Preface

The first step on the road to success is developing your personal definition of the word. Financial wealth is commonly associated with success; however, success is not limited to the wealthy.

Success may mean discovering a cure for cancer, or batting .500, or learning to utilize effective solar energy, or winning the Super Bowl.

I like the following definition:

> "Success is the orderly, ongoing advancement toward a goal – and the ultimate achievement of that goal. Success is arriving at that place where you have determined to arrive."

Perhaps one of the best known definitions of success is that of Mrs. A. J. Stanley:

> "What constitutes success? He has achieved success who has lived well, laughed often, and loved much; who has gained the respect of intelligent men and the love of little children; who has filled his niche and accomplished his task; who has left the world better than he found it..."

Success is ultimately a personal and private achievement. The final definition of **success** is one's own.

The man who assumes he will succeed without an understanding of what he wants, or where he is going, is doomed to failure. You cannot truly be a success without striving for and achieving **excellence** in whatever you choose to do.

The basic idea behind *Success and Beyond: 50 Keys* is that **success habits** are something that definitely can be learned. To be successful, a person cannot be accomplished in just one or two areas, while having great problems and difficulties in others. *SUCCESS AND BEYOND: 50 KEYS* says that a person must be well-rounded to experience total success. In the business world one must be aware of his entire surroundings – not just one or two things.

Knowing Eugene Swearingen as I have over the years, and after reading the manuscript, I realize the manuscript is the essence of Dr. Swearingen's life. In my personal opinion, Eugene Swearingen and his wife, Aasalee, are the epitome of success.

I know people who make more money than Swearingen, and I know many who make less. I know people who are more charismatic, and I know many who are less charismatic. But when it comes to being well-rounded and as close to putting it all together as is possible, this man and his wife have come closer to fitting that description than anyone I know.

Eugene Swearingen has been a success financially. He has been successful as a business leader, a church leader, a spiritual leader, a counselor, and as an example to thousands of young executives around the world. Each person he has had contact with has likely learned that success is more than just one or two techniques; that being a well-rounded individual is absolutely essential to success.

Many of the motivational book writers appear to have a lot of philosophy and very little personal experience in the area. As you read this book you understand that Swearingen has experienced and knows first-hand the people he mentions. The experiences are real, and the book shows how he personally gained insight as he handled many different situations.

I recommend *SUCCESS AND BEYOND: 50 KEYS*. It is my

opinion that as each reader develops each **Key** in his or her own personality, a level of personal fulfillment can be reached that no financial gain can approach.

Go For It! This book can change your life.

Rick Setzer
Greenville, South Carolina

∞∞∞∞∞∞∞∞

Don't sell yourself short. Stretch your vision. Get the big view of your life. Don't worry about trivial things. All things are possible to them who believe. Start believing big dreams.

Get yourself prepared to accomplish things that you have never thought possible before. Set measurable goals. You can succeed. People do it all the time.

~ *Eugene Swearingen*

Dr. Eugene L. Swearingen

"It was August 2nd, 1944 in the North Atlantic, 1,000 miles east of the Newfoundland Coast. I was on the U.S.S. Fiske, DE-143, a destroyer escort chasing submarines. We found two instead of one. We were making our run on one submarine, and the other came around to the side.

Our whole ship blew up. The bow sunk in 15 minutes. There were no life boats floating in the water. I was in the North Atlantic for five hours waiting to be rescued. My main thought was whether we would be picked up before night." – E. Swearingen

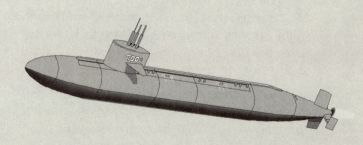

Success and Beyond: 50 Keys

Ensign Eugene L. Swearingen • 24 years old
United States Navy

Since serving his country, Eugene Swearingen has dedicated his professional life to the areas of education, business and finance. He has mentored thousands of young people and consulted for many enterprises, equipping them with these **50 Keys of Success** necessary to remain afloat and thrive in today's competitive environment.

DR. EUGENE L. SWEARINGEN

TABLE OF CONTENTS

KEY #1	God Designed You to Succeed	18
KEY #2	Limitations Make Great Lemonade	20
KEY #3	Keep Your Sponge Wet	24
KEY #4	As We Sow, We Shall Reap	24
KEY #5	Develop a Good Self-Image	28
KEY #6	Use Horse Sense to Cooperate	30
KEY #7	Act as if It Were Impossible to Fail	32
KEY #8	Decide What You Need to Do and Do It!	34
KEY #9	Learn to Read Others Like a Book	36
KEY #10	Find a Need and Fill It	39
KEY #11	Go the Extra Mile	43
KEY #12	Don't Give Up! Self-Discipline	46
KEY #13	Your Expectations Tend to Become Your Realities	49
KEY #14	Respect the Dignity of Every Person	51
KEY #15	Goals Will Change Your Life	53
KEY #16	Purpose and Happiness Come From Within	56
KEY #17	Don't Get Hardening of the Attitudes	59
KEY #18	Picture Yourself as You Want to Be	62
KEY #19	Get off Your Bottom to Get to the Top	64
KEY #20	Be Prepared for Change	66
KEY #21	Keep a Sense of Humor	68
KEY #22	Hold on to Your Good Health	70
KEY #23	Conquer Your Fears	72
KEY #24	God Made You to be a Winner	74
KEY #25	Ask and It Shall be Given	77
KEY #26	Enjoy Your Work	79

KEY #27	In a Race There May Only Be One Winner, But There Doesn't Have to be a Loser	81
KEY #28	Manage Your Time Well	82
KEY #29	Have an Inner Glow ....0............	84
KEY #30	Help Others Fulfill Their Needs and Dreams	86
KEY #31	Learn to Love people	89
KEY #32	Use "Persist-a-verance"........................	91
KEY #33	What Does the Sermon on the Mount Really Mean?	92
KEY #34	Get Outside of Yourself: Try Giving Yourself Away	94
KEY #35	Pick Your Associates Carefully	98
KEY #36	Be Dependable and Committed to Self-Improvement	101
KEY #37	Be Honest	105
KEY #38	Understand the Importance of Family	109
KEY #39	Manage Your Own Money	113
KEY #40	Keep Your Priorities in Balance	117
KEY #41	Demonstrate Courage	119
KEY #42	Learn to Speak Effectively	121
KEY #43	Use Good Manners	124
KEY #44	Become a Good Communicator	126
KEY #45	Develop Your Human Relations Skills	132
KEY #46	Become a Problem Solver	134
KEY #47	Know How to Give a 60-Second Praise	137
KEY #48	Know How to Give a 60-Second Reprimand	141
KEY #49	Be Enthusiastic !	143
KEY #50	Learn to Think Big................................	145
KEY NOTES	....	147
FINAL KEY COMMENT	....	151

KEY #1

~ GOD DESIGNED YOU TO SUCCEED ~

All of our talents come from God. Very few of our abilities result from our own effort. For the most part our brain functions, our organs function; and we grow and develop all for some unknown reason. I recommend two excellent books: *Be The Person You Were Meant To Be*, by Dr. Jerry Greenwald, and *Be All You Can Be*, by David Augsberger.

The Bible contains a Book of Acts, but does not contain a book of good intentions. If Paul had only **intended** to set up churches in the surrounding countries, little would have happened. It was only because he acted that we have such literature as the Letters to the Thessalonians, the Letters to the Romans, and so on.

Ethel Waters, the brilliant singer, said, "God didn't make no junk when he made me." I think God did not intend to make junk of any of us. I think God wants us to become the very best persons we can possibly become with the talents He has given us. Why would God want failures? I am sure we would not have been given these talents unless we were expected to use them in the very best way. And this means using them to become as successful in life as we can possibly be.

William H. Cook, of Bartlesville, Oklahoma, has

defined success as "The progressive achievement of worthwhile goals." He says that success is more than money; it is becoming the right kind of person.

It is not so much what God calls us to **do**, as what He calls us to **be**. I am convinced that God wants us to be successful in every phase of our lives – spiritually, physically, with our families, and even in regard to those material things we want and can use to improve ourselves and others.

We talk much about luck and chance. But I am convinced that we make most of our own luck, and we create our own opportunities. The world is marvelously ordered. I have read that watermelons have an even number of stripes, that oranges have an even number of segments, and that even wheat has an even number of grains on each stalk.

Aerodynamic engineers have proven that it is impossible for the bumblebee to fly because it is so poorly constructed. But the bumblebee doesn't know this, and so it flies.

Much of what has been given to us is simply beyond comprehension. Take the heart muscle as one single point of evidence. The heart is a muscle only about 6 by 4 inches, and it beats some 70 times per minute. Each time this muscle pumps it moves approximately 2 ounces of blood. This would exceed 7 tons of blood per day. The Psalmist said: "I will praise Thee, for I am fearfully and wonderfully made."

∞∞∞∞∞∞∞∞∞∞

> *All that I have seen teaches me to trust the Creator for all that I have not seen.*
>
> *~ Ralph Waldo Emerson*

KEY #2

~ LIMITATIONS MAKE GREAT ~
LEMONADE

Despite the fact that God has given us fantastic talents and abilities, even those of us who are in good health must recognize our limitations and accept them with good grace. All of us have to live with them. True, we tend to build on our strengths rather than our weaknesses; but some people have been able to turn weaknesses into strengths.

I came from a family in which the men in the family were tall on my father's side, but short on my mother's side. I always wanted to be more than 6 feet tall. However, I turned out to be 5 feet 8 inches tall. I didn't like it, but that's the way it was!

Once, I went in for a medical examination and the nurse said, "Stand up here, I want to measure and weigh you." I said, "You don't need to measure me, I am 5 feet 8 inches tall. I don't like it – but that's the way it is." She said, "Stand up here," and when she measured me she said, "You are 5 feet 7 inches tall." I said, "That's impossible, I have always been 5 feet 8 inches," and she said, "You are shrinking!" She explained further that when one becomes older one's cartilages begin to collapse and one actually does become shorter. So here I am, always having wanted to be 6 feet tall, and I am moving in the wrong direction!

When I was in the fourth grade all the boys and girls were required to be in the Choral Club. When the teacher first heard me sing, she told me that my voice was changing, and that if I were to sing in her Choral Club it would strain my voice, and might damage it forever. She exempted me from Choral Club and sent me to the library. The same thing happened in the fifth grade, the sixth grade, the seventh grade. I never did get to sing!

Most of you have heard of Terry Fox, and many of you have seen the movie. Terry Fox was a Canadian cancer victim. He was 22 years old when he discovered that he had only a short time to live. He decided that he wanted to raise money to aid cancer research. In order to attract attention to this cause, he attempted to run across Canada on his artificial leg. He had lost one leg to cancer.

As he ran from the eastern part of Canada to the west, more and more media coverage was generated, and he became a national figure. People came from the cities to meet him and run with him. Unfortunately, he was forced to halt the trip across Canada when it was found that cancer had spread to his lungs. Nevertheless, in that final period of his life, Terry Fox raised $24,000,000 to aid cancer research.

Ashby Harper, age 65, swam across the English Channel. The channel is approximately 21 miles wide where he crossed it, and it took him 13 hours and 52 minutes. It was estimated that Harper actually swam between 30 and 36 miles because the tide kept carrying him away from land. When Harper was asked why at age 65 he would attempt such a feat, he simply said, "I wanted people to know that just because they were 65 years old, life did not have to end."

A fantastic man named Michael McKern lives on what he calls "full tilt boogie." McKern is a drag car racer, an airplane pilot, a motorboat operator, a scuba diver, and has sailed across the Pacific alone. This story would not be particularly unusual except that McKern has no arms. Instead, he uses prosthetic arms with mechanical hooks. Despite this handicap he has lived a fuller and richer life than have most of us.

Louis Lourmais was a cancer victim who swam 217 miles down the St. Lawrence Seaway. He is blind in one eye and has lymphatic cancer. He made this swim just to demonstrate that cancer victims can still do many things that we would normally not think of them as being able to do.

A few years ago three paraplegics climbed Mount Guadalupe, the highest peak in Texas. It is said to be 8,751 feet high. These three men, Donnie Rogers, Joe Moss, and Dave Killey, not only made it to the top of the peak, but **all were in wheelchairs**. Three others tried and two of those almost made it to the top.

The *Reader's Digest* published a story of a climber who was caught on a mountain during a terrible storm. As a result of frostbite, he lost both feet. But this very determined man had mechanical feet made and has since climbed more difficult mountains than most of us would ever attempt.

Jackie Robinson was a great baseball player in the minor leagues. But he was black, and no black player had ever played in major league athletics. Branch Rickey in 1947 gave Jackie his chance, and he became the National League's "Rookie of the Year."

Wilma Rudolph was the twentieth of 22 children. She was stricken with scarlet fever and double pneumonia at age 4 that left her left leg paralyzed. The doctors said she might never walk again. But by age 10 she was walking; by 13 she was playing basketball; and at 20 she won three gold medals in the Olympics. She said, "It took a lot of work, discipline, and sacrifice, but it was worth it."

Twenty-nine-year-old Rick Hansen recently completed a 25,000 mile trek around the world in a wheelchair. As tears streamed down his cheeks, 40,000 admirers cheered him on his return to Vancouver following his 26-month adventure in a specially designed wheelchair. Spectators lined the final 20 miles of his journey and waved yellow "Welcome home!" ribbons. Hansen raised more than $10 million on behalf of the disabled on his journey, which began March 31, 1985, and took him to 34 countries.

Hansen met with presidents and prime ministers, was honored by Soviet officials in Moscow and was cheered by a crowd of more than 500,000 in China. Israel and Jordan granted him special permission to cross the Allenby Bridge between the two nations. Hansen played high school basketball until he lost the use of his legs at 15 when his spinal cord was severed in a car accident. Think of him the next morning your mind tries to tell you you're too tired to exercise.

∞∞∞∞∞∞∞∞

In the middle of difficulty lies opportunity.
~ Albert Einstein

You may be, at this moment, standing right in the middle of your own 'acres of diamonds.'
~ Earl Nightingale

Key #3

~ Keep Your Sponge Wet ~

If we are to keep on growing, we must keep on learning. A good definition of learning is, "An experience that changes our behavior." In any given situation if one's behavior remains unchanged, you can say that one has not learned. When we cease to grow we are old. Some people **are** old at 25 and others are still young at 80. It is all a matter of **attitude**. The successful person is always learning, is always looking for new opportunities to grow, to develop, and to become a better and more effective person.

All growth requires some risk. Growth also requires effort. Growth requires that we get out of our comfort zone. When our tolerance for discomfort is too low our growth is greatly limited. Until one is willing to get out of his comfort zone, he is not going to become a better person.

Don't worry about not having enough opportunities in life. When fate closes one door, faith opens another one. Opportunities never become exhausted, because every time we seize one, at least one more appears.

Once while I was in Hawaii, an article appeared in the papers concerning some unemployed persons. One man who had applied for employment said that all he could do was wash cars. The caseworker said, "Then why aren't you washing cars?" The man decided that he would. And at the time the story was written he had five other workers washing cars for him.

Another story in the Hawaii paper was about a man who, when unemployed had reflected upon what it was that he really liked when he was young. What he really liked was to eat snow cones. So he decided to get a machine that would shave ice and he was selling $600 worth of snow cones in Hawaii each day. I don't know the markup on a snow cone, but it has to be at least 100 percent because all it is is shaved ice and syrup. If my calculations are right, he was making more than $300 per day.

Life is a constant pilgrimage. Paul says in Philippians 3, "I leave the past behind and with hands outstretched to whatever lies ahead I go straight for the goal." What we have to learn is that life is ever changing, and we can either grow or decay – we will never remain the same. Every day some of our cells die, and other cells are born. Every day one's mind is programmed for better or for worse. The decision is in one's hands. Keep your sponge wet every day!

∞∞∞∞∞∞∞∞∞

> Learning is wealth to the poor, an honor to the rich, an aid to the young, and a support and comfort to the aged.
> ~ Lavater

> It is easy to learn something about everything, but difficult to learn everything about anything.
> ~ Emmons

> Learning makes a man comfortable with the company he keeps when by himself.
> ~ Young

Key #4

~ As We Sow, We Shall Reap ~

You can harvest only what you plant. A farmer would never plant corn and expect to harvest wheat. Likewise, we cannot plant negative and harvest positive. If you plant pictures in your mind of being poor, you will always reap poverty. If you think of yourself as living in a ghetto with no chance for progress, you will remain poverty-stricken in the ghetto.

It comes as a great astonishment to some people that they cannot plant hate and harvest love. **As we sow, so shall we reap**. No greater truth is known to man. Therefore, for whatever we want out of life, we must first plant the seeds. The seeds determine what you are going to harvest. You can get back only what you have planted.

Benjamin Franklin said, "If you would reap praise you must sow the seeds, gentle words and useful deeds." James Allen wrote in *As a Man Thinketh*, "As the plant springs from, and could not be without, the seed, so every man springs from the hidden seeds of thought, and could not have appeared without them...." Allen continues, "Good thoughts bear good fruit, bad thoughts bad fruit. A man will find that as he alters his thoughts toward things and other people, things and other people will alter towards him.... The Vision that you glorify in your mind, the ideal that you enthrone in your heart – this you will build your life by. This you will become."

∞∞∞∞∞∞∞∞∞∞

Whatsoever a man soweth, that shall he also reap. ~ *The Bible, Galatians 6:7*

The season of failure is the best time for sowing the seeds of success. ~ *P. Yogananda*

He who sows, even with tears, the precious seed of faith, hope, and love, shall come again with joy, bringing his sheaves with him.
~ *Cecil*

KEY #5

~ DEVELOP A GOOD SELF-IMAGE ~
ACCEPT YOURSELF

Maxwell Maltz has written a fascinating book entitled *Psycho-Cybernetics*. In this book he develops many reasons why one must have a good self-image. A famous plastic surgeon, Maltz found that when he removed ugly scars from people's faces, it often changed their attitude towards life and improved their self-image. His most remarkable discovery was that sometimes he could remove the scar **without improving** the self-image of the person.

I know a lovely lady at the Bank of Oklahoma who lost more than 100 pounds of weight. She looked like a new person, but she told me that every time she passed a mirror she was startled to see a thin person reflected, rather than the fat person she had always been. She succeeded in maintaining her new weight and gradually began to accept a self-image of being thin.

Don't depend on uncertain luck. The longer I live, the less I believe in luck, and the more I believe in preparing oneself for opportunities. Everyday we have many choices. We can go on the path to the right, to the left, or forward. The choices we make tend to determine the kind of person we are becoming.

Luck is the way we explain the **success** of persons we don't like. When someone we don't admire is successful, we simply say he was lucky. This absolves us from all blame for being a failure.

We must have faith and hope. Hope is the expectation of something that has not yet happened, but is within the range of possibility. The more we **work** and the more **faith** we have, the luckier we become.

∞∞∞∞∞∞∞∞

As a man thinketh in his heart, so is he.
~ *The Bible, Proverbs 23:7*

What happens to us is less significant than what happens within us.
~ *Lewis L. Mann*

Whether you think you can, or you can't, you are right.
~ *Henry Ford*

KEY #6

~ USE HORSE SENSE TO COOPERATE ~

Early in his life, Dr. Jack Wilkes was a pastor of the First Methodist Church in Perry, Oklahoma. Later, Dr. Wilkes became mayor of Oklahoma City and president of Oklahoma City University. One Sunday Jack Wilkes came into our church and said he had observed that horses would line up head to tail and swat flies for one another. He said that if horses had that much sense, surely the members of our congregation could cooperate. He said that he wanted to leave a poem with us. The poem goes: "When days are hot and flies are thick, use horse sense, cooperate. This is a truth all horses know. They learned it many centuries ago. One tail on duty at the rear can't reach that fly behind the ear. But two tails when arranged with proper craft can do the job both fore and aft."

It is said that the tide lifts all the boats. Teamwork is particularly important in corporate life. But it is also important in our families and our friendships. Cooperation is often more fruitful than competition.

A story is told of a man who died and was given the choice of going either to heaven or hell. He said he had never seen either place and would like to inspect both before he made a choice. He was taken down to hell. He saw a table covered with food, but every person had one arm strapped to his or her side and the other arm had splints tied so that the persons could not bend their elbows. They were starving to death despite available food, for they were unable with either hand to reach their mouths and feed themselves. They then took the man up to heaven and exactly the same situation occurred. The only difference was that the people were feeding one another.

Cooperation makes sense in almost every phase of our lives. Together we can do many things we cannot do individually. We must not only be able to cooperate with others, but we must expect their cooperation, and we must give them praise and glory for what they have done. People will not continue to cooperate with you if you expect to receive all the acclaim.

If you are going to be successful in a corporation, it is vitally important to develop a perception that you are a team player. Few great goals are reached in modern society by the work of an individual. It almost always takes cooperation.

William O. Douglas said, "A corporation director must think not only of the stockholder but also of the laborer, the supplier, the purchaser, and the ultimate consumer. Our economy is but a chain which can be no stronger than any one of its links. We all stand together or fall together in our highly industrialized society of today."

The mule can't kick and pull at the same time; neither can you. If you are pulling the oars, you won't have time to rock the boat. It is easy to employ people to work **for you**. What is hard is to find people that will work **with you**. The latter takes a commitment of the mind and the heart.

KEY #7

~ ACT AS IF IT WERE ~
IMPOSSIBLE TO FAIL

Make a habit of succeeding. A familiar adage tells us that we can learn from failure. But we can also learn from success – and it is much more fun. **Don't make excuses**. Nobody really believes excuses, anyway. They help only the person who makes them. What they really end up doing is making success more elusive.

Perhaps the most important single fact for us to learn is that we can deliberately program our subconscious mind. Medical experts tell us that every experience we ever had is recorded in our brain. Even such things as the sense of smell at the time of an accident are recorded. Even though we can't always retrieve this information, it is there in our subconscious and it influences our behavior.

One day while I was Chairman of the Board of the Bank of Oklahoma we had a meeting of the senior staff people. At this meeting one of the men used what I regarded as a vulgar expression. A woman officer was present. After the meeting I summoned the man into my office and told him that I did not sanction the kind of language he had used in the meeting. His response was, "It just slipped out." My answer to him was, "If it had not been in your mind it would not have slipped out."

Each of us individually must accept the responsibility for programming our subconscious. Negative thoughts occur to everybody, but if we allow these negative thoughts to linger in our minds and to dominate our thinking, it is our responsibility. We have the power of choice. God has granted us the power to reject things from our minds that should not be there and to accept things into our minds that should be there.

When you set out to accomplish anything, you must act as though you have already achieved your desire. So many of us say, "I am going to do something when I get around to it." Zig Zigler has a little coin he distributes that looks like a nickel but is described as a Round Tuit. Zig says that he passes out these coins because he is always getting the excuse that, "I intend to do it, just as soon as I get around to it." Now you have a Round Tuit.

Helen C. White said, "There is no failure so great that a Christian cannot rise from it, there is no defeat so final that he cannot convert it into a victory."

Failure takes no effort. It is about the only thing you can achieve without effort. It is **failure to try** that should be condemned. If you like what you are doing you will probably succeed – not fail.

Charles Kettering, the brilliant auto magnate said, "The one time you don't want to fail is the last time you try." Kettering added, "Learn how to fail intelligently...it is one of the greatest arts in the world."

∞∞∞∞∞∞∞∞

> Now faith is the substance of things hoped for, the evidence of things not seen.
> ~ *The Bible, Hebrews 11:1*

Dr. Eugene L. Swearingen

KEY #8

~ DECIDE WHAT YOU NEED TO DO ~ AND DO IT!

Don't procrastinate. Almost everything we put off doing is because of some emotional reason. Perhaps it is fear of failure, perhaps it is because we think the job will be distasteful. But whatever the reason, we can know mentally that it should be done; and still emotionally we do not allow ourselves to get on with the job of doing it.

One of the most important principles of success is that of **delayed gratification**. Almost everything worthwhile in life comes after considerable effort. If you like to be paid daily for what you have done, then mow lawns! At the end of every day you will have some money in your pocket, and you will have instant gratification.

The really successful people, though, are those who are willing to work now to be paid later. In other words, they are willing to make an **investment** of their time, their money, and their abilities.

It is said that several million men last year bought a $1/4$-inch drill. It was not that they wanted the drill or the bit; what they really wanted was a series of holes. If you want the holes you have to buy the drill. This is a necessary investment for doing the job well. And you expect to make the investment **before** you receive the return from your efforts.

William Cook says, "Delay an action once, and the chances of getting it done diminish. Delay it several times and we may never do it."

People who succeed do so because they are willing to do the things that failures won't. For any task, the first question to ask is WHY should it be done. It is only after we have decided **why** it should be done that we go about determining HOW it should be done.

Someone has said, "Too many people set their goals based on where they have been, rather than where they want to go." Thomas Huxley said, "The most valuable trait you can acquire is the ability to: (1) Make yourself do what you should. (2) When it ought to be done. (3) Whether you like it or not."

Procrastination is a device of the devil. It prevents us from doing what we know we should do. And in many cases it results in never getting the job done. The inevitable result is that we end up being less successful in life than we could have been if we had simply learned to act when the time was right.

Frances Rodman said, "Always put off until tomorrow the things you shouldn't do at all." But the things you know you should do, do them today. Benjamin Franklin said, "You may delay, but time will not."

The only things we should put off until tomorrow are the things we should not do at all. Prioritize what you should do. Do the most important things, and either delegate or ignore those of lesser value.

Key #9

~ Learn to Read Others ~ Like a Book

We have all heard of body language. We recognize that people communicate with us through body language, but we sometimes forget we also communicate to others through body language. A blink, a smile, or the crossing of one's arms are all a part of body language. Freud said, "The unconsciousness of one human being can react upon that of another without passing through the conscious." What this really means is that my subconscious, primarily through body language, can be communicating with you; and your subconscious may be transmitting messages to me of which you are totally unaware.

When I went into the banking profession, I was told that an old Cantonese proverb says, "Watch out for the man whose stomach doesn't move when he laughs." Often, when I was facing a loan applicant I realized that many gestures and even words are artificial. When a man really laughs his stomach does move. But when the laugh is artificial his stomach probably will not move. Therefore, what the Cantonese proverb is saying is, "Watch out for the man who is telling you a lie."

We have almost no written description of the physical Jesus. But what we do have is a whole series of references regarding the impact He had upon people. I am convinced that Jesus must have had the most penetrating eyes of any man ever to live. We all know that women, especially, communicate with their eyes. One can see love or hate, anger or affection, all by looking into the eyes of another.

In banking, and in fact all sales work, we teach people to watch the prospect's eyes. When the eyes are downcast, and when the face turns away, you are being shut out. But if the mouth of the prospect is relaxed, his chin is forward, and he looks enthusiastic, then you are well on the way to making the sale.

I told our bank officers that they will never make a loan when they are leaning back away from the applicant. I have noticed that when a loan presentation is made, if the officer of the bank really wants to make the loan, he tends to lean forward; he often unbuttons his coat, and in some cases he will remove his coat and relax to hear the rest of the story.

When people are under severe stress their hands betray their emotions. When their hands are made into a tight fist we read apprehension or anger or fear in the gesture.

I am told that during World War II our American spies were trained to cross their legs in the European style rather than the American style. American men tend to cross their legs by forming a figure four. That is, they will let the ankle or calf rest on the other knee. European men fully cross their legs.

For those of you who are interested in learning more about body language I heartily recommend a book entitled *Learn To Read Others Like a Book*, by Nierenberg and Cabero.

Someone has said that 50 percent of the interview is

over when the applicant sits down. What this means is that first impressions are acutely important. Unfortunately, we have only one opportunity to make our first impression. The way a person dresses and walks into the room, the eye contact, the handshake, and the appearance of poise or lack of poise are determined during the first few minutes of an interview.

While I was President of the University of Tulsa, I interviewed an applicant for the head of one of our engineering departments. During our first interview the applicant sat and looked out the window most of the time we were talking. For some reason he simply could not establish eye contact with me. Obviously, I was not impressed, and he was not hired for the position.

> The tree is known by his fruit. Out of the abundance of the heart the mouth speaketh.
>
> ~ The Bible, Matthew 12:33,34

KEY #10

~ FIND A NEED AND FILL IT ~

One of the most successful couples I know are Ed and Mary Malzahn, of Perry, Oklahoma. Ed went through Oklahoma State University in engineering and returned to Perry to work with his father in a machine shop. One day Ed Malzahn realized that ditching machines were moving a lot more dirt than was necessary for the size of pipe being laid. Ed set about to fill a need. He developed the world's best ditching machine, which he called the "Ditch Witch."

Perry is a town in northern Oklahoma of approximately 5,000 population. It would seem an unlikely place for one to become a multimillionaire. But Ed and Mary Malzahn set about building the finest ditching machine on the market, and today their annual sales approach $185,000,000 at retail. This represents approximately two-thirds of all the ditching machines sold in the entire world.

It is interesting that this success story was accomplished without any significant government help, without low-cost loans, and without the community subsidizing his efforts. In fact, it is not an overstatement to say that the prosperity of Perry, Oklahoma, depends upon one man who employs some 800 people, and who is one of the most socially responsible businessmen I have ever known.

Do you feel you deserve to be rich? An almost automatic law determines that you will never receive from life much more than you feel you deserve. Many people are willing to talk the talk, but are not willing to walk the walk. By this I mean that many people are always talking about doing something great, but never find the appropriate time. Only those who have dreams, and then put these dreams into action, realize their full potential. Most of us go through life accomplishing only a fraction of what God intended.

A prime question to ask yourself is, "What level of earnings do I want for my family?" I believe you should deliberately determine where you want to be 1 year from now, 3 years from now, 10 years from now, and at the time of your retirement. You have tremendous God-given potential, but unless you are careful, most of it is going to be wasted. Using this potential takes planning, goal setting, and motivation. Are you willing to pay the price for success?

I know that success can be defined in many ways, and each person must develop his own definition. But there is no reason why we should set out to achieve failure. By failing to plan, we are planning to fail.

Dr. Dennis Waitley says, "Winners are those individuals who in a very natural, free-flowing way seem to consistently get what they want from life by providing valuable service to others."

A businessman I greatly admire is Bob Parker, Sr., Chairman of the Board and Chief Executive Officer of Parker Drilling Co. It has been my good fortune to be both his friend and business associate. I have learned much from him. Bob is technically one of the best in the oil field drilling business. But that is not really the secret of his success. Bob Parker inherited a broken-down drilling company from his father at a time when the industry was in chaos.

He began to analyze the need for oil and gas throughout the world. He became convinced that most of the easy places to find oil and gas had already been discovered. He knew that much of the oil and gas distributed over our world had to be in places quite inaccessible to the usual drilling equipment. **He saw a need and filled it!**

One of his employees, Ted Houck, not a highly educated man, but a real genius, designed a drilling rig that would drill deeper than 25,000 feet and which could be divided into parts small enough to be carried by helicopter, by boat, by canoe, even by mule pack if necessary, to any part of the world.

Parker Drilling Co. is now the largest onshore drilling company in the world, with rigs scattered all over the map. Parker is drilling on the North Slope, the jungles of Peru, the swamplands of Indonesia, and every other conceivable place where oil and gas might be found.

The final point I want to illustrate is that no man can become rich by himself. Ed Malzahn has become rich out of the Ditch Witch machine. But so have many other people who assisted him in the company. Bob Parker has literally produced a dozen or more millionaires. He, of course, has become a multimillionaire. But he didn't do it without assistance. Andrew Carnegie once said that it is impossible for a man to become rich without making others rich.

∞∞∞∞∞∞∞∞

Ideas control the world.

~ Garfield

The measure of someone is the number of people whom he or she serves.

~ Paul D. Moody

KEY #11

~ GO THE EXTRA MILE ~

Vince Lombardi produced a film called, "The Second Effort." In this film he used replays from some of the Green Bay Packer games. The point Lombardi was trying to make is that in every play shown in the film it looked as if the play was over but the whistle had not blown. Through a tremendous **second effort**, the person carrying the ball was able to get out of a pile of people, or do something else dramatic, that enabled him to go for the touchdown. In life we have two options: we can either strive for our possibilities, or we can settle for others' probabilities.

At the time of the Chicago fire hundreds of businessmen had gathered to watch the fire, which was out of control, and to see their businesses destroyed before their very eyes. For most of them, this was a disaster. But Marshall Field had a different attitude. As he saw the fire, he said to himself, "Tomorrow is going to be the best time in the world to buy land in this area. I will buy up the land that is available, and I will build the biggest retail store in the world on this site."

In the church I've seen a number of people who believe that striving for success is somehow sinful. I have seen others who believe that making money is contrary to the will of God. I personally have a very different concept of God. I believe that God wants all of his children to be as successful as they can possibly be. Why would God give us talents that he would not expect us to use? Why would God want His children to be poor, while those who reject Him are rich? Why would God want us to be anything less than the very best that we can be?

Henry Ford, Thomas Edison, Martin Luther King, Winston Churchill, and Mohandas Gandhi were all **great dreamers** who never considered giving up. They made the second effort, the third, or whatever it took to be successful. They were all **committed** to a cause. The ordinary person **becomes extraordinary** when he has a vision, a purpose, and a goal. The Bible says, "Without a vision the people perish."

I remember the year we went down to see the Dallas Cowboys play the New Orleans Saints. The Cowboys were behind by seven points. With only two minutes to go in the game it looked as if victory was impossible. The New Orleans Saints were about ready to score again – some of the people were already beginning to move out of the stands – when the Saints decided that they would kick a field goal. They tried the field goal and Ed "Too Tall" Jones blocked the kick. The ball went back behind the kicker, a Cowboy grabbed it and ran for a touchdown, leaving them just one point behind. They missed the conversion, so they were still one point behind.

Everybody believed that the Cowboys had lost the game. Then suddenly, when they kicked off, they were back in the game – New Orleans was back near the goal line. The man carrying the ball was tackled behind the goal line for a safety. The Cowboys got two points and won the game by one point.

The amazing thing is that it's this **second effort** – the belief that the game is not over. All of those eight points were scored in the final two minutes of the game when it looked as if the Cowboys could not score.

An enterprise, when fairly once begun, should not be left till all that ought is won.

~ Shakespeare

The harder you work, the harder it is to surrender.

~ Vince Lombardi

Key #12

~ Don't Give Up! ~
Self Discipline

One thing all successful people learn is to hang in there. It is told that when Thomas Edison was trying to develop the incandescent light bulb, one of his co-workers came to him and said, "Mr. Edison, we have had 5,000 failures." Edison responded, "No, we now know 5,000 things that will not work." Soon after that, Edison tried using tungsten as the filament for a light bulb and it was successful. Today we have light bulbs all over the world because Thomas Edison refused to accept a series of failures, but instead kept on trying to become successful.

One of the most successful marketing men in America is Dexter Yager. Dexter is a popular speaker and writer and is author of a recent book entitled *Don't Let Anyone Steal Your Dream*. This book has sold more than a half million copies, and the principal theme of the book is don't give up. **Never – Never – Never – Quit!**

A few years ago I was watching the semifinals of the NCAA Basketball Tournament. It became apparent that the game was going to be decided in the last minute. If you watch athletic games you will see that in many cases the game is simply a matter of inches. The team that has the greatest desire is the one that usually wins. The team that folds under pressure is always a loser. Tom Landry said that in a football game only six to eight plays really make the difference. The only trouble is we never know in advance which six or eight plays they are going to be.

Henry J. Gray, Chairman and Chief Executive Officer of United Technologies, ran a full-page ad in *The Wall Street Journal*, January 12, 1984, in which the message was, **"never give up."** I have reprinted the ad from *The Wall Street Journal* because I believe it is applicable to every line of endeavor, and to every reader of this book.

> "Is that what you want to do? Quit? Anybody can do that. Takes no talent. Takes no guts. It's exactly what your adversaries hope you will do. Get your facts straight. Know what you're talking about. And keep going. In the 1948 Presidential election the nation's leading political reporters all predicted Harry Truman would lose. He won. Winston Churchill said, "Never give in. Never. Never." Sir Winston stuck his chin out and wouldn't quit. Try sticking out your chin. Don't give up. Ever."

Babe Ruth was known for his record of 714 home runs. He was "the home run king." Not so well known is that Babe Ruth also set an all-time record of 1,330 strikeouts. People wanted to see Babe Ruth hit a home run. They were not concerned about how many times he struck out.

It is easy to steal the dreams of your wife, of your husband, or of your children. We do not want those dearest to us to be hurt. Therefore, we sometimes wish that they would not try to succeed. But we must recognize that no progress is ever really made without some risk. We have to leave our **comfort zone**. Dr. Dennis Waitley says, "When you hit a sour note, finish the song before you start another."

We have a grandson named J. Paul. On one of the last days of summer J. Paul went off the high dive at Southern Hills Country Club in Tulsa, when he was only four years old. The following summer we were going for our first swim, and Paul said that he was going to go off the high dive. His mother, Sandra, said, "Paul, you'd better be careful, you may get hurt." I said, "Sandy, you may have just set him back several months." Predictably, Paul did not want to go off the high dive; we spent the rest of the summer getting him back to the point where he had ended the year before.

It is so easy for us unintentionally to steal another's dreams. A cynical remark or even the look in our eyes may communicate to the other person that we do not believe he or she can succeed. Such communication tends to make the person fearful of failure and less likely to reach his or her full God-given potential.

It's so hard when I have to, and so easy when I want to.

~ *Sondra Anice Barnes*

KEY #13

~ YOUR EXPECTATIONS TEND ~
TO BECOME YOUR REALITIES

Joe Batten and I have worked on a number of management development programs for Gulf Oil Company. Joe is one of the most creative, dynamic human beings I have ever known. He has recently written a book entitled *Expectations and Possibilities*. In this book, in his lectures, and in the films that he has produced, he develops the theme that we tend to get from ourselves no more than we expect. We get from our employees only what we expect. And many of our potential possibilities are destroyed because of a lack of expectation.

I am told that there have been experiments in which children were divided into three groups as nearly alike as possible with respect to learning ability. One teacher was told that she had the outstanding learners. The second teacher was told that she had the average learners, and the third teacher was told that she had the slow learners. Remember, all of the classes were as nearly identical as possible.

After 90 days the rate of learning among these children was measured and somehow the teacher that expected great things from her class had the highest

Dr. Eugene L. Swearingen

rate of learning. The teacher who thought she was teaching average students, in some unexplained manner, communicated to them that they were average. Unfortunately, the teacher who thought she had the slow learners also communicated to them the fact that she did not expect a high level of performance from them.

If we expect the best from ourselves, and we expect the best from our employees, that is what we tend to get. Our families would be greatly improved if all of us would learn that we must have high expectations of one another if we are indeed going to be successful.

We tend to get what we expect.

~ Norman Vincent Peale

Life tends to respond to our outlook, to shape itself to meet our expectations.

~ Richard DeVos

KEY #14

~ RESPECT THE DIGNITY ~
OF EVERY PERSON

As a manager it is necessary for you to judge the performance of employees, particularly those employees who report to you. It will be your responsibility to recommend some for promotion and to recommend pay increases, merit increases, and so forth. So there is no escaping the fact that you must judge the **performance** of your people. But that does not mean that you judge your **people**.

Christians have trouble with the fact that the Bible says you should not judge other people. Well, we are not supposed to judge other people, but we do have to judge their performance. And there is a difference. A person may not perform well on an examination, but that does not mean that the person is inferior. We don't know what kind of problems might have caused that person not to perform well on the exam. We do know that the performance was unsatisfactory. But that does not mean that the person lacks worth. And so what we have to learn is that we judge people's performance, yes; but we do not judge other people.

I used to tell people at the Bank of Oklahoma, "It is

all right for you to turn down a loan, but do not turn down the person who applies for the loan." By this I mean that a person who comes in to borrow money from the bank quite often is a little bit fearful. He or she is uneasy about whether the loan is going to be granted. As a bank officer, you can turn down a loan in such a way that that person will never return to the bank.

On the other hand, if you have to turn down the loan, you can do so in such a helpful, considerate manner, giving worth and dignity to the person, that he or she will love the bank. And when the person qualifies for a loan, he or she will want to come back and do business with you. So it's important to turn down the loan, but not the person applying for the loan. There's a poem that goes like this:

> I dreamed death came the other night, and Heaven's gate swung wide.
>
> With kindly grace an angel ushered me inside.
>
> And there to my astonishment stood folks I'd known on earth,
>
> Some I'd judged and labeled as unfit – of little worth.
>
> Indignant words rose to my lips, but never were set free
>
> For every face showed stunned surprise – not one expected me!

∞∞∞∞∞∞∞∞

KEY #15

~ GOALS WILL CHANGE YOUR LIFE ~

I believe you should set goals in every area of your life. You should set physical goals for your health. You ought to set spiritual goals. You should set material goals. You should have family goals. You should have goals with respect to your church and community activities in which you want to engage – all areas of your life need goals.

If you have not been a goal setter, learn to be a goal setter. Put God in your goals. Let God help you determine what is worthy of your best efforts.

I do not feel that there's anything wrong with Christians wanting money. In fact, I feel that it's a rather perverted attitude to believe in a God who would want His children not to have the best things in life. To me there is absolutely nothing wrong with having money provided your priorities are right.

As the Bible says, the **love** of money is the problem. Loving money to the point that it's more important to you than anything else can be a very real problem. Having your priorities mixed up on how you spend money can also be a real problem. But I think there is nothing wrong with making all that you can, as long as you make it honestly and ethically and morally. Then I think you ought to **save** all you can, and you ought to **give** to other people and to the church all that you can. This is essentially what Calvin and John Wesley both said – that there is nothing wrong with being successful. It is simply that you need to be successful in a way that will still keep straight your priorities with God.

Money in itself is not evil. In fact, I have found that the people who are most hung up on money are the people who do not have money. Not having money in our society can be a very damaging experience. In the bank I've seen people go bankrupt. I've seen people who were really hung up on money simply because money had become all powerful to them. But my experience is that the people who have a lot of money – provided their priorities are right – can do many good things. And they do. I've seen people give liberally to charity and to other worthwhile causes.

I hope that in every area of your life you will set goals. These goals should be measurable. They ought to be something you can visualize. They ought to be something that you can quantify. And you must have a time period on them. Write them down. It does not do any good to say, "I'm going to read more books" and not set a date for completion. If you put dates on these goals and they are measurable, then at the end of the time you can say you either reached the goals or didn't reach the goals. And this can be very challenging.

Not reaching the goal by the specified date does not mean you are a failure, or that the goal was bad. Don't abandon the goal. A good goal is still a good goal. Maybe you need to revise the plan. Or maybe the plan is good, but will just require a little more time than you thought. Knowing what your goals are and being motivated to reach them are important. But without **action** nothing will happen. **Doing something** will move you toward your goals.

∞∞∞∞∞∞∞∞

You can plant a dream.
　　　　　　　　　　　　　　~ Anne Campbell

The big thing is that you know what you want.
　　　　　　　　　　　　　　~ Earl Nightingale

The world has the habit of making room for those whose words and actions show that they know where they are going.
　　　　　　　　　　　　　　~ Napolean Hill

Key #16

~ Purpose and Happiness ~
Come from Within

The great myth is that happiness depends upon external factors. The truth is most people are happy not because of things that happen **to** them, but because of things that happen **within** them.

When you accomplish goals that you have established and that you feel are worthwhile, you feel good and you are happy. People who are constantly seeking happiness from external factors seldom find it. People who find happiness are the people who decide to do something worthwhile. When they accomplish the goal they suddenly find that, "Sure, I was happy. Why wouldn't I be happy? You know, I was having a good time. I was delighted. I was making progress. I was successful."

Consequently, this type of experience lends purpose to your life. When you have a purpose for living and when you accomplish something that you consider worthwhile, then you are going to be happy. I think the statement that John F. Kennedy will be remembered forever for is, "Ask not what your country can do for you, but what you can do for your country." This type of challenge, **getting outside of yourself**, becoming bigger than you are, is going to make you happy. You will never be happy just by going someplace else. Many people try to find happiness in other parts of the world. They travel from one resort to the other. They go every place. But my experience is that you are not going to be happy someplace else if you're not happy where you are. And so, if you're happy now, then you can be happy elsewhere. Dennis Waitley said:

> "Happiness then is a natural by-product of living a worthwhile life. It is not a goal to be chased after or sought."

Maxwell Maltz has written a small but very valuable book entitled *Five Minutes To Happiness.* He describes the purpose of his book as that of teaching the art of being happy. He believes that happiness is habit, just as worry is. He spells out the pitfalls to be avoided that make one unhappy and describes the steps you need to take each day to be sure that you are happy.

We have all been endowed with the ability to make choices. We can choose to be happy or we can choose to be sad. I am told that it takes far fewer muscles to smile than it does to frown. A smile is contagious. If you smile, then others are likely to respond by smiling. We can decide to be cheerful, or we can be hateful. We can be friendly toward other people, or we can treat them with anger and lack of compassion. We can be critical of others, or we can be tolerant. **The choice is up to us.**

Happiness is a state of mind in which we have pleasant thoughts most of the time. No one is happy all of the time. Every human being faces problems and stress. But we can choose to follow the happiness habit or we can choose to be an unhappy person. For those of you with a tendency toward depression, I recommend a book entitled *Happiness Is A Choice*, by Frank Minirth, M.D., and Paul Meier, M.D. In this book the authors discuss the magnitude of suicide and some of its causes. It seems strange that some people would deliberately choose to be unhappy. But these authors believe some people do make such a choice in order to punish themselves for guilt feelings.

∞∞∞∞∞∞∞∞

Happiness is not pleasure, it is victory.
~ *Zig Ziglar*

Happiness is not in having or being; it is in doing.
~ *Lilian Eichler Watson*

Happiness does not come from doing easy work but from the afterglow of satisfaction that comes after the achievement of a difficult task that demanded our best.
~ *Theodore I. Rubin*

Key #17

~ Don't Get Hardening of ~ the Attitudes

Your attitudes can be either real assets for you or real liabilities. **You** are the only one who can determine what your attitudes are going to be. No one else should have control over you and your personality. One of the most important attitudes is the attitude that you have toward yourself. Your **self-image** is vitally important and few people succeed with a negative self-image.

Enthusiasm is another attitude that is highly communicable, and people like to be around others who are enthusiastic. If you are a leader, you want enthusiastic followers. If you are a sales manager, you want enthusiastic salesmen. If you are an athletic coach, you want enthusiastic players.

Your attitude toward the people with whom you work is extremely important. In almost all corporations, you must get the job done either through other people or in cooperation with other people. Your attitude can make other people feel important or unimportant. Your attitude can make people either want to work with you and for you or against you.

When you feel important, you are much more likely

to make other people feel important. Helping others to achieve what they want out of life is a sure way of getting more of what you want out of life.

If your attitude toward people is that every person is important, you will find it easy to remember his name. Every person likes to hear his or her name, and every person likes to believe that he or she is important enough that you will remember who he or she is. When you fail to remember a person's name you are indicating that you did not consider it worthwhile to learn their name. Consequently, every successful politician learns very early in the game that people like to be called by their names. The successful politician puts this to work to show others that he appreciates what they are doing on behalf of his or her campaign.

Another attitude Jesus stressed was the attitude of service to other people. Many people like to be the **boss** but do not really like the role of **servant**. But Jesus stressed that he who wants to be the highest in a group must become the servant to that group.

Your age is not really important, but your attitude about your age is extremely important. There are people who are only 30, but because of their attitudes they think and act as though they were 60. There are other people who are 60, but because of their attitudes they think and act as though they were 30 years old.

Do not ever think that it is too late for you to do something. Many people have taken up painting late in life. I had never really painted until I reached my sixtieth birthday. The children asked what I wanted for a birthday present and I told them to get me some oils, I was ready to start painting. They said, "Whom are you going to take lessons from?" I told them that I didn't want to take lessons, I wanted to do my own thing.

I have found painting extremely relaxing, and for me it has been a wonderful outlet and diversion. I know that I am not a great painter, but I didn't start painting to produce works of art. I started painting because I wanted to paint, and I felt this way of expressing myself would be enjoyable.

William James, a famed psychologist, said, "The greatest discovery of my generation is that human beings can alter their lives by altering their attitudes of mind." Inspiration, perseverance, and belief will be more important in your life than knowledge. Dennis Waitley wrote in a book called *The Winner's Edge* that everything is in attitude. Not **aptitude, but attitude** is the criterion for success.

∞∞∞∞∞∞∞∞

No one can make you feel inferior without your consent.
~ Eleanor Roosevelt

People are disturbed not by the things that happen, but by their opinion of the things that happen.
~ Epictetus

Any fact facing us is not as important as our attitude toward it, for that determines our success or failure.
~ Norma Vincent Peale

Key #18

~ Picture Yourself as You ~ Want to Be

In the Bible, Mark 11:24 says, "Therefore I say unto you, what things soever ye desire, when ye pray, believe that you receive them, and ye shall have them." Paul Myers says, "What you ardently desire, sincerely believe in, vividly imagine, enthusiastically act on, must inevitably come to pass." Emerson said, "Thoughts rule the world." William James says, "Belief creates the actual fact. Think love and you will be loved." Proverbs 23:7 says, "For as he thinketh in his heart, so is he."

We tend to become what we think. It has been said, "All that we are is a result of what we have thought." Jonathan Edwards said, "The ideas and images of men's minds are the invisible powers that constantly govern them." And Dr. Norman Vincent Peale said, "Think success, visualize success, and you will set in motion the power force of the realizable wish." When the mental picture is strongly enough held, it actually seems to control conditions and circumstances.

M. R. Kopmeyer, in his book entitled *Here's Help*, says, "Your future will be what you mentally picture it will be." Think poor, and you'll be poor. Think goodwill, and you will attract goodwill. Think cowardly thoughts, and you will become a coward. Think hateful thoughts, and you will be filled with hate. Think love, and you will be filled with love.

Your subconscious mind is extremely important in determining your behavior. We must realize that our subconscious is constantly being filled with mental images. Even more important, we can control the kind of mental images that enter into our subconscious. If we begin to picture ourselves as successful, we will become successful. If we begin to picture ourselves as failures, we will be filled with fear and all of the problems relating to fear will be brought down upon us.

Your subconscious is subject to **your programming**. You have control of your mind – no one else should have this control. You are responsible for what you imagine, and for what you dream. You are responsible for what you read, and for what you allow to be brought into your subconscious. The desires that we have tend to become wants, and then needs, and finally what we desire tends to direct our course of action. Dreams have a way of coming true because they transform a wish into concrete action. Thoughts are not just things that happen by chance into our minds. We should be in control of our thoughts, and we can decide how to program our minds so as to be successful.

Picture yourself as a success, as a winner, as fulfilling all that God has made possible for you to become.

Dr. Eugene L. Swearingen

Key #19

~ Get Off Your Bottom ~ to Get to the Top

One of the reasons people fail is that they give up too soon. Persistence is necessary for success in almost all endeavors. People who will not get up and get started are called procrastinators. They are unwilling to do what they know they should do, and instead they give all sorts of excuses and alibis for their failure to perform.

Many successes in life require specialized education. One gets this specialized knowledge by reading, or by enrolling in university programs, or by on-the-job training. We will never be successful until we learn not to blame others for our mistakes. Accepting criticism for a job poorly done is a necessary part of learning to do the job well in the first place. Wishing that something will happen is almost never enough. Success requires action. So get off your bottom and get started.

A friend, C. C. Hope, who was President of the American Banker's Association, enjoys telling a story about this hound dog, Ole Blue. He has a dozen or more of these stories. One of them is of Ole Blue howling one day, and a man who had walked into the country store asked the manager, "What's wrong with Ole

Blue today?" And the manager said, "Well, he's sitting out there in a sticker patch." "Well, why doesn't he move?" the man asked. And the manager said, "Because he'd rather howl."

Now, sometimes we have these people in business. I've seen some of them both in universities and in banks – people who would rather complain than to do something about it – people who would rather howl than to say that they appreciate what's being done for them. If you're going to be successful you have to get up and get going. You should have a dream worthy of your life. Everything we read in the Bible teaches us that we must first exert effort. If we want something, we have to first provide some action to achieve it.

It is better to wear out than to rust out.

~ Cumberland

Sloth makes all things difficult, but industry all things easy.

~ Franklin

God has so made our mind that a peculiar deliciousness resides in the fruits of personal industry

~ Wilberforce

Dr. Eugene L. Swearingen

Key #20

~ *Be Prepared for Change* ~

New ideas, new knowledge, new value systems. We are constantly exposed to change in our environment. We have new approaches to old problems, new goals and aspirations and new commitments. There's a story of a 90-year-old man who was having his birthday party, and a guest said to him, "You must have seen a lot of changes in your life." And he said, "Yes, and I've been against every one of them."

People like this are constantly opposed to change, and yet the fact that they are opposed to it doesn't prevent its happening. Maurice Chevalier, the popular Frenchman, was once asked: "Do you resent having birthdays?" And he said, "I did, until I considered the alternative." Now once you consider the alternative to having birthdays, you decide it's probably better to go ahead and have birthdays.

Change is not easy. And as we grow older we tend to resist change. But some people manage to accept change when they're 80, and other people tend to resist change when they're 25. So change is not necessarily related to age. We can condition ourself to be the kind of person who can accept change and who can even benefit from change.

Almost everyone fears change and yet almost every change brings good things to **some** people. Change may bring bad things to some other people, but some people benefit from change because change is almost always initiated by somebody. It doesn't just happen.

∞∞∞∞∞∞∞∞∞

*I*n this world of change naught which comes stays, and naught which goes is lost.
~ Mdm. Swetchine

*I*t's the job that's never started that takes longest to finish.
~ J. R. R. Tolkien

A *work well begun is half ended.*
~ Plato

Dr. Eugene L. Swearingen

Key #21

~ Keep a Sense of Humor ~

It is important to be able to laugh at yourself. I have learned that one of the best ways of starting off a speech is to tell a joke in which you are the victim. It is not recommended, for example, if you are Irish to tell jokes on Jewish people. If you are Jewish you may be able to get by with telling a joke about a Jewish person. But if you are Irish, you had better tell Irish jokes, because people resent denigration of people of other races or other religions. But if the joke is on yourself you can get by with it. Why? Because people like somebody who can laugh at himself – somebody who does not take himself too seriously.

I tell a story that I think illustrates the way people identify with a certain person in a story. This is a story of four persons on a train who sat in facing seats. One was a colonel, one was a private who'd been the butt of the colonel's jokes all day long; a third was an old maid, and the fourth was a young and beautiful blonde.

The conductor came through the train with the announcement, "We're going into a tunnel pretty soon, and the electricity is off in the train." He said, "It'll be dark momentarily, but don't be too concerned because the tunnel isn't very long."

Well, they entered the tunnel and it became pitch dark. Soon they all heard a kiss and then a sharp slap. As they left the tunnel, they were all very curious as to what had happened. The colonel's face was crimson. It was quite apparent that he had been slapped.

The colonel thought to himself, "Now, I've been dealing with a very clever private here today. And he was smart enough that when we went into the tunnel, he kissed the blonde and I got slapped for it." Well, the old maid did not like the colonel but she did like the private, and so she thought that the colonel was the kind of guy who would take advantage of this situation. She surmised that when they went into the tunnel he had kissed the blonde and he was slapped for it, and she thought this was a form of justice.

The blonde was only perplexed because she knew that she hadn't been kissed. She decided surely the colonel intended to kiss me; he got mixed up in the dark, kissed the old maid, got slapped for it, and this rather amused her. Only the private had the facts to reach the right conclusion. You see, he knew that when the train entered the tunnel he'd kissed the back of his hand and slapped the colonel.

People identify with the private in that story. Turn that story around and have the colonel be the winner, and people will not think it's funny. It's only when the private wins that the story is funny. So be able to laugh at yourself. Keep a keen sense of humor.

∞∞∞∞∞∞∞∞

KEY #22

~ HOLD ON TO YOUR GOOD HEALTH ~

It is sad, but true, that we do not really appreciate good health until we no longer have it. And many of our health problems are due to abuse of our bodies. Smoking, excessive alcohol, lack of exercise, obesity, anorexia, stress, lack of sleep, improper eating habits, and now drugs, are all dangerous to our health. But the important thing is that **all of these are, or should be, in our control**.

In the spring of 1987 I learned how important my health was. One day when I was supposed to chair an important meeting, I simply could not get going. I cancelled the meeting and went to my Internist. After examining me, he put me in the hospital. After further tests they installed a pacemaker. While lying there in bed, I began to seriously consider what was really important to me in life. We have all the material things we need. My family, my friends, and my health were the only things really important. For Betty Ford, it was alcohol and drugs that were the problem. For me, it was obesity, stress, and lack of exercise. I decided there in bed on my back, that I was going to do something about it.

Two weeks later I was at the National Institute of Fitness in Ivins, Utah. (Phone number 801-628-3317.)

This fitness resort is one of the very best – not a luxury spa, but a real health program which changed my life. I lost 25 pounds in six weeks and 6 inches in my waist. But more important, I am changing my lifestyle. The Institute has an excellent program for weight (fat) control, nutrition, and fitness. I believe that this program will add **years of quality** to my life.

Dr. Mark and Vicki Sorenson, of N.I.F., have dedicated their lives to helping others reach their goals in health and fitness. Losses of 50 to 100 pounds are not uncommon. The best part is you are not on a diet. Your fitness comes from exercise and good nutrition, **and the weight loss is usually permanent.**

Decide today that you are going to do something about your health. Whatever your health problem, you can do something about it. But first you must make the **mental** commitment. Second, you find the program you need to make the change. Then you begin to change your bad habits into good ones. Christy Lane sings in *One Day At a Time,* "Lord, for my sake, teach me to take, one day at a time. Yesterday's gone, sweet Jesus, and tomorrow may never be mine. **Lord, help me today, show me the way, one day at a time.**"

Joy, temperance and repose, shut the door on the doctor's nose.
~ *Longfellow*

Health is the greatest of all possessions.
~ *Bickerstaff*

Dr. Eugene L. Swearingen

KEY #23

~ Conquer Your Fears ~

Fear of failure can predispose you to failure. Some people worry about everything in the world, yet most of these things they worry about never really develop.

Fear can keep you from being a good manager. One of the most important facets of being a good manager is to be able to delegate. But if you fear that people will not perform, or if you fear that **they** are going to get the credit, or if you fear that they might appear to be even better than you are, then you're not going to be willing to delegate jobs to your subordinates.

This is going to mean that your subordinates cannot grow. And it's also going to mean that you cannot be an effective manager over a large operation. You can manage a large business **only if you delegate**. If you are fearful, you will find it very difficult to delegate. And so, what you must do is discard the fear of failure, fear that somebody might look better than you are, fear that somebody else is going to get the credit.

Fear causes us to settle for less than we can be. I hope you think of yourself as being better than average. Because average is the bottom of the top, and it's the top of the bottom. Average really doesn't mean very much. If you are nothing more than average, in the sense that you are in the middle, perhaps you should be at the top. Average is not good enough. You can do better than that. You can do better than that simply because God gave you the capacity to do better than that. You have the ability. It's just a matter of using that ability so that you can accomplish more.

Nobody trips over a mountain, only little rocks. If you think about it, most of the problems we worry about and most of our fears never materialize. The problems are not very important, and yet they may get in our way. Someone has said, "**If you fall, fall forward** and at least gain that much." Get up and get going!

∞∞∞∞∞∞∞∞

> *There is no fear in love; but perfect love casteth out fear.*
> ~ The Bible, I John 4:18

> *Nothing in life is to be feared. It is only to be understood.*
> ~ Marie Curie

> *Action conquers fear.*
> ~ Peter Nivio Zarlenga

DR. EUGENE L. SWEARINGEN

KEY #24

~ GOD MADE YOU TO BE A WINNER ~

I believe that God gave all of us talents to grow and to develop and to be winners. I do not believe that God wants His followers to be failures. Why wouldn't He want each of us to be just as successful as anybody else? And even more successful! After all, if we are followers of God, then it seems to me with that source of strength, we ought to be able to at least do better than average. Consequently, we should not settle for being a loser.

On August 2, 1944, I was on a destroyer escort and we were chasing a submarine. Instead of one, we found two! And one of them came in from the side and sank us. I happened to be the officer on the fantail of the ship and a number of crewmen with broken legs were around me. Their legs, by the way, were broken when the deck went up, not when they fell down.

A man named Johnson was sitting on the deck. He was not an ordained minister, but every Sunday morning he had led a service on our ship. Both of his legs were broken. I asked him if I could help him, and he said, "No, help the others. God will take care of me." And do you know that five hours later, I was pulled out of the water, and the first person I saw upon deck was Johnson. How he got there, I haven't the slightest idea;

but I do know that a lot of our people died of shock. They were injured, but had no reason to die except for **fear** and the length of time in the water. We were straight east of Newfoundland, so it was pretty cold in the water. The combination of cold water, shock, and fear caused a number of our people to die. There was no reason, physically, why they should have died. The men on each side of me were killed in the explosion. I was not touched. One wonders, "Why not me? Why them, and why not me?"

I am convinced that when tragedy strikes, Christians are not necessarily spared. I saw Christians die that day and I saw other people, who I at least thought were not so good, survive. But I do know this. I saw what happened to Johnson because he believed.

What I really feel is that God gives us the ability to meet whatever challenges come. This does not mean that we are going to be spared suffering and other problems. I don't think Christians are exempt from accidents. We're going to have tragedies and health problems in our families as are non-Christians. Christians can get cancer just as non-Christians can. But I do believe the main difference is not in what happens to us, but in our resources to deal with any kind of problem.

Learn to pray regularly. Don't blame God for being where you are. Instead, pray for His help in arriving where you want to go. I believe that it is vital to focus on a goal where you want to be three years from now, five years from now, and on down the road. I hope that after reading these **50 Keys**, all of you will become goal setters. I hope you'll also become persons who habitually cut out pictures of things you want and put them on your refrigerator door.

I have found that setting goals, writing them down, putting them where you can see them, will remind you constantly of where you want to be, and then you will tend to move in that direction. Dennis the Menace asked himself, "How can I be lost if I don't care where I am?" Well, if you don't care where you are, how can you be lost? God provides us with virtually unlimited possibilities. We have to make a choice from among all the possible things that we can become. We have to choose what we're going to become. We have to choose where we want to be. We have to choose how we're going to get there. Then we have to pay the price for success.

∞∞∞∞∞∞∞

> *The battle of life is, in most cases, fought uphill; and to win it without a struggle would be without honor. If there were no difficulties, there would be no success; if there were nothing to struggle for, there would be nothing to be achieved.*
> ~ Samuel Smiles

> *You make up your mind before you start that sacrifice is part of the package.*
> ~ Richard M. DeVos

> *The smile of God is victory.*
> ~ Whittier

KEY #25

~ ASK AND IT SHALL BE GIVEN ~

In the Bible, John 15, verse 7, reads, "If ye abide in me and my words abide in you, ye shall ask what ye will, and it shall be done unto you."

Earlier I mentioned my good friend, Joe Batten. His company runs about 5,000 management/development programs a year. Every time he autographs a book, he writes, "Expect the best, Joe Batten." "Ask, and it shall be given you; seek, and ye shall find; knock, and it shall be opened unto you." (Matthew 7:7) If you read the New Testament, you will find that asking is a very important part of getting. You have to focus upon what it is you want. If you don't ask for it, you may not get it.

One of the reasons we do not ask is that we do not believe we are deserving. Matthew continues, "For everyone that asketh receiveth; and he that seeketh findeth; and to him that knocketh it shall be opened."

It is God who is our source. God wants us to be successful, but our goals must be worthy. We will not ask unless we believe. To believe we must have faith. St. Augustine said that to find God one must first "believe that he will eventually find Him."

To me, Matthew 7:7 is so direct, so powerful, so conditional, that it is unbelievable that Christians do not pray for their needs to be met. Perhaps our self-image is so low we cannot ask in faith.

∞∞∞∞∞∞∞∞

If ye...know how to give good gifts unto your children, how much more shall your Father in heaven give good things to them that ask Him.
~ The Bible, Matthew 7:11

Whatsoever ye shall ask in prayer, believing, ye shall receive.
~ The Bible, Matthew 21:22

Whatsoever things ye desire, when ye pray, believe that ye receive them, and ye shall have them.
~ The Bible, Mark 11:24

KEY #26

~ ENJOY YOUR WORK ~

The Apostle Paul wrote, "Everyone be sure that he is doing his very best. For then he will have the personal satisfaction of work well done and won't need to compare himself with somebody else." Did you know that the word 'work' appears some 574 times in the Bible. There would not be a New Testament of any significance had there not been a Book of Acts. It is not our good intentions, but what we do, the action that we take, that is important. And **work** is a very important part of everybody's life. It should be important in your life.

I tell young people, if you don't like what you're doing, for heaven's sake get out of that and do something else. You will not be successful at doing something that you intensely dislike. I can't imagine any worse life than to have to spend eight hours a day for the rest of your life doing something you dislike. If you get into something you like to do, then you will be successful. If you get into something you don't like to do, you will not do it well and you will not be successful. Therefore, find something in your life that you consider worthwhile and uniquely you, that is a challenge, that you **want** to do, and that you **enjoy** doing. That is a wonderful discovery, if you ever make it.

The problem is that we do not have enough hours left in the day to really enjoy life if we don't enjoy our work. Most people will work more hours than they spend for recreation, at least until age 65. The industrious person with average I.Q. will pass the lazy person with a superior I.Q. It is not so much your intelligence as it is your ability to apply that intelligence.

The person who does not work for the love of work but only for money is not likely to make money or to find much fun in life.
~ Charles M. Schwab

I never did a day's work in my life. No matter how difficult, it was all fun.
~ Thomas A. Edison

You don't pay the price for success, you enjoy the price for success.
~ Zig Ziglar

Key #27

~ In a Race There May Only ~ Be One Winner, But There Doesn't Have to be a Loser

I like to get involved in races without any losers. I think one reason people like the Boston Marathon is that everybody who finishes wins. I know people from Tulsa who've gone to Boston, not with the goal of winning, but with the goal of finishing. Being able to finish is really laudable. In the annual Tulsa Run, it doesn't make any difference how far or how fast you can run; it's just being a participant that counts. Participation can be a highly enjoyable thing; and people really get something out of being involved. I like the kind of competition in which everybody wins. Some kinds of competition are like that, if you simply look for them.

In service organizations, everybody can win by raising money for a charity. I've seen people really get out and compete, but everybody wins. There are no losers in raising money for the Red Cross, which we did recently in Tulsa. We raised about $6 million. We serve 37 hospitals out of the blood bank in Tulsa. Everybody who worked on the campaign was a winner, not a loser.

Timothy said, "I have fought a good fight and I have finished my course. I have kept the faith."

KEY #28

~ MANAGE YOUR TIME WELL ~

In **KEY #8** I quoted Thomas Huxley who said, "The most valuable trait you can acquire is the ability to make yourself do the things you need to do when they ought to be done, whether you like them or not." **Failures** are people who just don't feel like doing it. How many times have you heard people give an excuse, "Well, I would have done it, but I just didn't feel like it." "I would have taken that course in continuing education, but I just didn't feel like it." "I didn't get around to it." (See again **KEY #7**)

Program your time. None of us has extra time, but everybody has some time. Nobody can get any more time. I am told that the world is slowing down on its axis, and that 3 million years from now there will be a 25-hour day. Until then, there are 24 hours. Nobody can get any more; nobody has any fewer.

The one excuse I will not accept for not working for one's community is that one simply doesn't have enough time. When I was campaign chairman of the United Way, I would call people and ask them if they would head up a division. And some of them would say, "Gene, I'd love to, but I just don't have the time to do it." I would say, "Look, anybody I ask is going to have 24 hours a day, **no more**. Now if you want to tell me that the United Way is not high on your priorities, that you are not concerned with whether Tulsa has agencies that serve needy people, if it is low on your priorities and you want to admit to it, fine. But don't tell me you don't have time, because you have the same time that anybody else I ask is going to have, and it's just a matter of how you set priorities on the use of your time. If you think it's important enough, then you'll do it."

I have heard it said, "If you want something done, ask a busy man to do it." One reason for this is that busy men learn to program their time. They **have** to learn to program their time. Busy men learn that 10-minute intervals are important. You think that the time you lose is all in blocks of three hours or more. It isn't! The time you usually lose in 5-minute intervals, 10-minute intervals, times you just squander. Not lengthy periods, but a multitude of goof-offs add up to a whole lot of time. That's how we really lose time. For example, when someone calls on you in your office, if you want to keep the conversation short, simply remain standing. We simply fail to use time effectively.

∞∞∞∞∞∞∞∞∞

Don't serve time; make time serve you.
                              ~ *Willie Sutton*

Plan your work for today and every day, then work your plan.   ~ *Norman Vincent Peale*

KEY #29

~ HAVE AN INNER GLOW ~

Let me relate some qualities I like to see in people. Good will. Alertness. Excitement. Enthusiasm. If you haven't read Norman Vincent Peale's book, *Enthusiasm Makes the Difference*, by all means read it.

Oral Roberts has told me that he rereads two books every year: the Bible, and a book written by Frank Betger entitled, *How I Changed Myself From Failure To Success in Selling*. Frank Betger's primary sales tool was enthusiasm. Read that book. I recommend it to you.

Exhilaration! Elation! Confidence! These are qualities I like to see in people. Anticipation! Radiance! Faith! Love! When I was younger, there was a movie entitled *The Magnificent Obsession*. That movie prompts me to ask you: **What is your magnificent obsession?** What is it that you really want to accomplish in your lifetime? What is your dream? What is it you really want to be remembered for?

Cheerfulness is said to be "the window cleaner of the mind." There is no question that cheerfulness and a positive attitude help create good health. The late Norman Cousins demonstrated that laughter can improve your body. Stress, worry, anxiety, and fear all contribute to sickness.

Being a person of good will is a choice you can make. You control your attitudes, your emotions, and your subconscious. Don't let anyone else take control of your behavior or your feelings.

∞∞∞∞∞∞∞∞

A merry heart doeth good like a medicine: but a broken spirit drieth the bones.
~ The Bible, Proverbs 17:22

Good nature is the very air of a good mind; the sign of a large and generous soul, and the peculiar soil in which virtue prospers.
~ Goodman

Key #30

~ Help Others Fulfill Their ~ Needs and Dreams

Often in management development programs that I have directed, somebody has complained about his boss. "Everything is fine in my company, except my boss!" Quite often I have asked them, "What does your boss really want out of life? What turns him on? What motivates him?"

Do you know, most people have never asked themselves what motivates their boss? They don't care what he wants out of life. So I suggest to them that one of the best ways of getting along in any organization is to go back and find out what it is that your boss wants out of life and **help him get it**. Doesn't that make sense? If you help him get what he wants out of life, he's going to help you get what you want out of life.

Most people who are having trouble with their boss are concerned that he isn't worrying enough about what **they** want. They are not concerned about what **he** wants; it's what they want that counts! Go back and find out what your boss wants out of life, and help him get it. If you help him get it, then I think he'll help you get what you want out of life.

Try to discern what other people need and what their wants are; help them get it, and this will make you friends. All sorts of good things will begin to happen to you, and you will certainly have more acceptance by other people if you simply help them get what they want. Many people just want some attention. They'd like to be recognized as an individual. They would like to be thought to be worthy of some attention. Ego needs are extremely important for most people.

Most of us have taken care of our physical needs. Most of us have shelter and all the food we need. Some of us eat too much. We have our basic needs supplied. What many people lack is a good self-image. They do not feel good about themselves. They don't feel that they are attractive. They need strengthening of what I call the ego needs. They need to feel that they belong to a group, that they have friends, that they're accepted. You can give them these things at a very low cost to you just by simply showing them some attention. Being admired, being appreciated, and feeling worthy of attention are all important.

My wife and I have four wonderful grandsons and one granddaughter. Everyone of these has said, "Look, Papa Gene, look at me!" They want me to look at them because they want to feel important. I don't care whether it's diving off the diving board or whatever it is, "Look at me!" Every child says that. When we get to be adults, we learn that we don't say, "Look at me!" But as a matter of fact, we really still need that kind of attention.

Where do you get this kind of attention? I hope that

you get it in your family. I hope you get it in your church. I hope you get it wherever you work. I hope you get it in the friends you choose. I hope you get it in the University you attend. Because if you don't get it in those places, I don't know where you're going to get it. Those are the places where we really ought to find love, where we ought to find a feeling of worth about ourselves. And in all of those places, people should care. And by caring, I mean they care about **me**. That's what we are interested in.

Our true destiny is not to be ministered unto, but to minister to our fellow man.

~ Franklin Delano Roosevelt

The highest of distinctions is service to others.

~ King George VI

And whosoever of you will be the chiefest, shall be servant of all.

~ The Bible, Mark 10:34

KEY #31

~ LEARN TO LOVE PEOPLE ~

Dr. Carl Menninger said, "Love cures people – both the ones who give it and the ones who receive it."

I read a book a few years ago written by a young seminarian who said, "I suddenly realized that I loved God and hated people." And then he said, "I realized I was going to be leaving soon and taking over a pastorate. And I realized I wasn't ready to take over a pastorate." You know, some people can do a brilliant job preaching in the pulpit, but aren't worth a dime as a pastor when it comes to actually going out and dealing with people one-on-one and working with them in this way. I've seen some other people who were wonderful in the pastoral relationship, but not very good when it came to getting up and delivering a sermon.

Develop this ability to love people, to show interest in people; and I'm not talking about how to win friends and influence people. I don't recommend **some** self-help books. I think to some degree what they are really teaching us is how to **manipulate** people, to make them do what we want them to do. I do not believe in manipulating people. I think that what we ought to be doing is showing interest in other people. Real interest, not spurious. If we have real interest in people, it will show through. On the other hand, if it's feigned, I think they will eventually see through us. Jesus first loved us and taught us how to love other people, so Christians have a wonderful example to follow about what love really means.

It is very hard for some people to demonstrate love. Some families do not demonstrate love easily. The idea of even touching one another is frowned upon. In some families, touching just comes naturally. In Italian families they really do this. Also, in Greek families and many others this comes naturally. But in some families people have great difficulty showing love even when they have it. I know some parents who have great difficulty telling their children that they love them. And yet, that may be what the children need more than anything else. A lot of people that I know in business settle for giving their kids money. They feel that when they've done that they have fulfilled their parental duties. That is **not** enough! Children need something more than that. They need to feel safe, feel that they belong, and feel that they will be truly loved regardless of what comes.

∞∞∞∞∞∞∞∞

Honour thy father and thy mother: and, thou shalt love thy neighbor as thyself.
~ The Bible, Matthew 19:19

You will find as you look back upon your life that the moments which stand out, the moments when you have really lived, are the moments when you have done things in a spirit of love.
~ Henry Drummond

KEY #32

~ USE "PERSIST-A-VERANCE" ~

"**Persist-a-verance:**" that combination of **Persistence** and **Perseverance** that pays rich dividends (I know it's not in the dictionary, but it's one of my special words for success). J. Paul Getty said, "There are three ways of making money. One is to inherit it. One is to marry it. The third is to find something that works and duplicate it." He then said, "The secret of success is to try harder." And he added, "The harder you try, the luckier you become." I really don't believe that much of our success or failure in life is owing to luck. I believe much more of it is owing to what finally comes out of us in wisdom and attitudes. I think desire, action, and faith are much more important than luck in determining success.

In trying times, too many people stop trying. Robert Schuller has made famous the saying that tough times never last but tough people do. In his book, *Tough Minded Faith for Tender Hearted People,* Schuller says, "Faith is climbing your way out and up, and **climbing** is spelled **w-o-r-k-i-n-g!**"

It is said, "Pray as if it all depends on God, and work as if it all depends on you!" All through the Bible you will find approval of the good worker – the one who tries harder – and disdain for the lazy. Make your life more productive and it will be more rewarding.

Key #33

~ *What Does the Sermon on the* ~ *Mount Really Mean* ?

For me this is one of the more difficult passages in the Bible. But I am sure that those people who are poor really learn the value of life. Blessed are those who are poor. Blessed are those who have great difficulties, because they will have great motivation.

I am amazed at the number of successful people who will tell you that they came out of very poor families. It seems to me more people who have made it on their own come out of poor families than come out of rich families. Maybe that's not unusual because there are more poor families than there are rich families. Nevertheless, I think that if you are poor, humble, and oppressed you will have more motivation to succeed.

I went to Tonkawa Junior College in Oklahoma because the tuition fee for a semester at that time was $7.50. At Oklahoma State University, it was $12.50. The $5 made a difference to me. Three of us rented a garage for $5 a month. We slept in that garage, cooked, studied, and did everything else. It had an open fire that really never bothered us as far as gas escaping because there was a gale coming through most of the time from underneath the door of this garage. We didn't have a door. The whole front end just lifted up! I remember one day some girls came to take a church census. They asked us what our names were and we said, "Swearingen, Stackhouse, and Cooprider," which was true. And they said, "Now look, this is serious business; you tell us the truth!" But it was the truth!

People who have difficulties do not have as much trouble getting out of their **comfort zone** as some of the rest of us. One of the problems many of us have in starting on a new phase of our life is that **we already have it too easy**. We aren't motivated by another car, because we already have a pretty good one. We aren't motivated by money, because we really don't have any real money problems. People can be in a **comfort zone** that is so comfortable that they'll just sit and watch television, letting the world go by, and not start on any new endeavors at all simply because it involves getting out of this comfort zone and taking some risks. Every change that you have in life, every new job you accept, every new challenge that you have involves taking some risk. Nevertheless, get out of your comfort zone. Don't settle for mediocrity. Be the best you can be!

∞∞∞∞∞∞∞∞

B*lessed are the poor in spirit: for theirs is the kingdom of heaven.*

B*lessed are they that mourn for they shall be comforted.*

B*lessed are the meek for they shall inherit the earth.*

~ *The Bible, Matthew 5:3-5*

Key #34

~ Get Outside of Yourself ~
Try Giving Yourself Away

There is a book by that title and I recommend it to you. The author, David Dunn, has a chapter on postage stamp giving. He says, "If you think that you don't have enough money to help other people, I'll ask you this: Do you have enough money for a postage stamp?"

If you have enough money for a postage stamp, somebody that you know needs a letter from you. You ought to sit down and write that person and tell them how much they have meant to you. You could bring so much pleasure to people if you would just do this. And yet so many people don't even take the time to write their dearest friends.

I think that's one of the problems with the modern telephone. Instead of writing and telling people how much they mean to us, we've all gotten to the point we say we will call them on the phone. But we may even forget to do this. And so we may end up not giving very much.

Learn to help other people. If you want to have a friend, **then be a friend**. If you take every opportunity you can to help other people, you will have friends.

There are a lot of people who end up feeling that they don't have any friends, and I must tell you that, in most cases, they got exactly what they earned. If you have not been a friend to other people, then you probably are not going to have very many friends.

Before we set out to move the world, we ought to first move ourselves. If you want to get to the top, get off of your bottom (See **Key #19**). Mohandas Ghandi said, "You will find yourself by losing yourself in service to your fellow man."

I believe America is a great country because of the free enterprise system which we have. We are more free to choose our vocation than the people of any other nation in the world. We are more free to get an education. Almost anybody in America can get an education. We have so many educational programs, so many work opportunities, that most people can get an education if they want it.

I've counseled over 10,000 students and I've yet to have one come back and tell me that he or she got too much education.

One of the reasons I have a Ph.D. is because my father had only an 8th grade education. During the depression, he would write letters trying to get a job; and I remember the letters he got back saying, "We had to lay off people who were college graduates. We had to lay off people who were high school graduates. And you haven't graduated from high school."

That so ingrained in him a determination that his three sons were going to have a college education, that he just couldn't settle for anything less. One of the reasons that we all graduated (the other two brothers are petroleum engineers) was because my father **didn't** have that opportunity. He was raised in Western Nebraska during World War I, 15 miles from the closest high school. His father was "running" cattle during World War I and making money. And my grandfather saw no reason for sending my father off to high school. Consequently, he didn't get much education. But because he didn't get that education, he compensated by seeing that it was going to happen with his children.

America is great because we have great expectations. Almost all of us believe we are above average. Most of us believe that we are going to be successful. We believe that we have the chance to reach the top. And so, we endeavor to do just that. It is the expectations that we have which cause us to achieve success. If we didn't believe, then we wouldn't have those expectations. So belief has to come first. And belief comes primarily from the system which we're in.

You can look around you and see people who are accomplishing great things. *FORBES* magazine each year lists the people in the United States who are the wealthiest. As I remember, they list 400 people. The article has a short biography of each one of these people. About half of them inherited their wealth or married it. But the thing which was really important, **about half of them came from nothing**, literally nothing. They had one great idea. And because they had this idea, they became successful.

For one of them it was McDonald's hamburgers. As you read the story of those people, you understand why they became successful. For most of them, they simply had terrific drive, persistence, and determination; and they had at least one good idea during their lifetime. They parlayed that one good idea into a fortune.

Uncommon people are the products of uncommon dreams. But people who are successful, I am convinced, are of a different breed than the people who are failures. People who are successful are people who have strong desires, strong faith, strong determination, persistence, perseverance, and positive attitude. They are people who habitually win. Or if they lose, they learn something and try again. And because they keep on trying, they become people whose attitude is focused on winning. And that determines the way they start into a race.

People who are losers, unfortunately, can become habitual losers. Their attitude begins to be affected by the fact that they have lost so often. They have a very strong subconscious feeling that they are not worthy, that they are not winners.

∞∞∞∞∞∞∞∞

The deeds of charity we have done shall stay with us forever. Only the wealth we have so bestowed do we keep; the other is not ours.

~ Middleton

Give, and it shall be given unto you; good measure, pressed down...running over....

~ The Bible, Luke 6:38

Dr. Eugene L. Swearingen

Key #35

~ Pick Your Associates Carefully ~

It is said that if you want to be a big flea, you've got to travel on a big dog. If you want to catch the flu, what would you do? Hang around somebody that has the flu. If you want to catch the measles, hang around somebody that has the measles. If you want to catch positive ideas, hang around somebody who is a positive thinker.

If you want to learn how to make money, hang around people who've made money. Your broke brother-in-law is not going to be able to tell you how to make money. If he knew, he'd make some!

In the 16 years I taught economics, I never taught anybody how to make money. And the reason was, at that time, I hadn't learned how to make money. If you don't know how to make money, it's hard to teach other people how to make money. It's hard to teach something you don't know. Try teaching sometime when you're not prepared.

It is extremely difficult to be positive if you're around negative people. Therefore, pick your associates deliberately so that you're going to hang around winners. If you hang around losers, you're going to become a loser in attitude. If you do hang around winners, you're going to become a winner.

You young ladies, when you're picking a husband, pick a winner. I know that there are a lot of girls that think they can reform a loser. Let me tell you, that is not easy; and there are an awful lot of women that found it was impossible.

Some of the brightest young women I have known have a habit of picking losers, two or three of them. I mean, they have married several losers. I don't know why in the world they don't recognize that they're getting another loser. It makes a difference. You can pick a winner or you can pick a loser. It's up to you, you know!

The most important decision that anyone makes, man or woman, is picking the person you're going to marry. There is no more important decision that you will make in your entire lifetime. The only trouble is most people make it when they're too young. They need to have all the wisdom of an 80-year-old to make the right kind of choice. But they don't have it.

In a corporation, I encourage young people to look for a **mentor**. A mentor can guide you and help you develop and can give you visibility. Some of you know my namesake, John Swearingen. John Swearingen was Chairman of Standard Oil of Indiana. He was in the Tulsa office at one time and he was in the Oklahoma City office. But when he was in both of those offices, it was well known that a person who was high up in the company was his mentor and that he had been picked early for success.

He was picked ahead of time by a mentor who was capable of giving him the kind of exposure which made it possible for him to be selected President when the time came.

I did the same thing for Dr. Pascal Twyman. When I was President of the University of Tulsa, I picked Pascal Twyman as my vice president. I made him vice president for research. Pascal had an outstanding record at Oklahoma State University. He was handsome, intelligent and hard working. I knew that he was going to need to know the faculty, and I later moved him over to vice president for academic affairs. I got him involved with the students, because I wanted the students to want him for President when the time came. I groomed him.

I told Pascal when he came to the University of Tulsa that I would make him president of a university within five years. I didn't know it was going to be the University of Tulsa at that time, but I set about immediately to give him all the kinds of experience that would enable him to become the president of a good university. Of course, Pascal had great ability. If I had not believed in his potential, I would have been looking for another person with the potential to succeed me.

With the right kind of mentorship (or sponsor), you can get the kind of exposure that you need in a corporation. And a lot of people never get it. One other point, if you pick a mentor, don't pick one that's going to get fired later, because it's only while he's around that he can do you much good as far as **your** career path is concerned.

KEY #36

~ BE DEPENDABLE & ~
COMMITTED TO SELF-IMPROVEMENT

It is extremely important for you to have a reputation that you will do whatever you say you are going to do. Giving your word that you're going to do something and carrying through with it is extremely important.

I had a young man come before my banking class once from the Bank of Oklahoma. This young man, each month, handled in excess of one billion dollars for the Bank of Oklahoma. On the average day, he would buy more than one hundred million dollars worth of "Fed funds" from certain banks and sell them to other banks.

The Bank of Oklahoma both buys and sells in the federal fund market. These are not funds that belong to the government. These are funds which belong to other banks that do not need those reserves at the Federal Reserve Bank at that time, and so there is a market established.

In 12 years of banking, I know of only one case in which the people agreed on the telephone to a rate for this money and then one party reneged. The amazing thing to me is hundreds of millions of dollars every day are bought and sold on the basis of a telephone call. Now that is real reliability; and it says something, I think, about the character of the people that you're dealing with when you can have those kinds of transactions and do not have any problems.

Being reliable and being able to have people depend upon you is extremely important.

I like both **books and tapes**. I have some motivational tapes that I commend to you if you're interested in listening to tapes on how to be successful. They are available in good book stores.

I had my students in an executive development class that I taught for years, listen to some tapes that Dr. Dennis Waitley has done. Then they listened to tapes on time management. They listened to Napoleon Hill's "*Think and Grow Rich*," with Earl Nightingale doing the commentary. There are a lot of good tapes available.

You should listen to these tapes not once, but to the point that you practically know when you are playing it, what comes next. When you get to that point, the information on that tape is becoming a part of your subconscious, and it's going to influence your behavior. If you just listen to a good tape once and throw it away, I tell you that within a week you will have lost half of what is in that tape.

The really good ones ought to be listened to time and time again. I have a tape player in my car. During the time I am driving, I have two choices: I can either listen to the radio, or I can listen to tapes. And I tell you, I won't learn anything listening to the radio. And so, I listen to tapes. I strongly commend tapes to you. Become a **book and tape addict**.

Good tapes are a wonderful way to reinforce the positive. We get so much negative thrown at us every day. Sometime you should analyze a one-hour news program and find out how much of it is about rape, about murder, about everything that is negative that's going on in our society. And observe how little of the program ever tells about somebody who's doing a good job or doing something good. For example there may be a fireman who really deserves to be a hero. Look at what he did in the last fire. He got the children out! And that's not considered news.

We don't hear much about the good things that go on in our society. What we hear is just negative, negative, negative! I'm afraid that many families get to the point where they are negative in their marriage, they're negative with each other, their attitude is negative. Consequently, we need a lot of positive reinforcement to offset the negative.

The way to get positive is to program yourself so you can get that positive reinforcement. There are two good ways to get the right attitude. One is to read the right kind of materials; and second, listen to the right kind of tapes. If you have figured out a better way to get your head on straight, let me know, because I'm interested in any better way. I do know one other way and that is being around the right kind of people.

It is estimated that the average person uses about 7% of his or her brain cells. Even a genius, they say, does not use more than 10% or 12%. At any good university, we are in the business of causing people to become as near what God will let them become as possible. That is our job. What we are to do is to take all the talents that have been given to these young people and help them to develop so that they can become as near what is possible as they can. And if we can motivate them and lead them and guide them so that they do become an outstanding person, it's amazing how much growth they can have.

Whatsoever things are true, whatsoever things are honest, whatsoever things are just, whatsoever things are pure, whatsoever things are lovely, whatsoever things are of good report...think on these things.

~ *The Bible, Philippians 4:8*

The best bank collateral is character.

~ *J. P. Morgan*

KEY #37

~ BE HONEST ~

I know that there are some people who appear to succeed by cheating. I have not known people who succeed over a long period of time by cheating. To me, integrity makes a lot of difference. People with integrity are people with whom other people like to do business. People who lack integrity have to keep on the move pretty fast from one place to the other. Having integrity is extremely important.

I always told our employees in the bank, "We deal with tainted money. It tain't ours!" When you are dealing with other people's money, you have a special responsibility. And that means that banks had better hire people who are honest. But even in spite of the fact that we try to hire people that are honest, we lose $8 internally to every $1 that we lose to a bank robber. Do you get that? We lose $8 inside the bank to our own employees for every dollar that we lose to a bank robber!

Almost every kind of store, whether it be a food store or even a country club, can have a lot of money being lost out the back door by simply not having honest people. So I think we should be honest and trustworthy. Maybe we don't say enough about this. We just assume that people have integrity. Sometimes we're wrong, and this becomes a major problem.

For the past ten years I have been on the Board of Regents for Higher Education in Oklahoma. We are trying to get more and more money for education. In one recent year the only major element in state government that got more money was **prisons**. Now there's something wrong with a society where the new money, all the additional money, had to be put into prisons rather than into education or other worthwhile projects.

Let me tell you my own story about education. I believe that we have a responsibility to educate ourselves as fully as we can absorb education. I had the G.I. bill when I came out of the service, and I went to Stanford University to get a Ph.D. The government subsidized my education up to about $5,000 a year for two years. The government put about $10,000 into my getting a Ph.D. Now what kind of a deal did the government get? The deal they have is that out of every extra dollar I earn, they get fifty cents. And they have been getting it now for many, many years. Last year alone, they got much more than the $10,000 that they paid for my education.

If I could take some bright young people and put them through medical school and get even thirty cents for every extra dollar they earned, could I afford to do it? Sure I could! It would probably be declared slavery if I did it, but the government has that deal. So, I say the government can't afford not to educate people to have the highest productivity they can possibly have. The way the government shares in the receipts – increased productivity – increased tax revenues!

Honesty, trustworthiness, telling the truth. I will tell

you a story about what happened to me when I was at Oklahoma State University. We needed a head of the Department of Finance. I called a man at a fine university who was the dean, and asked him if they had anybody that they could recommend to head up a finance department. He told me, yes, they had a young man who was looking for such a position.

I brought this young man down, showed him Oklahoma State University, and talked to him about the possibility of his heading the finance department. The man was attractive, he was fluent, and he was obviously extremely bright. He had a Ph.D. from a good university. So I thought we had really found a jewel. I said, "Would you like to stay over tonight? I think we're going to offer you a job, and you might want to look at housing while you're here." He said, "Yes, I'd be glad to stay."

It happened that the accounting department was meeting that night. He went with me to this meeting. At this meeting we began discussing the CPA exam, evaluating how difficult it was compared to a Ph.D. Our guest said, "Well, really the CPA is not too difficult." He continued, "When I was in the service in Ohio, they were giving the CPA exam, so I just took it to see how hard it was. I passed all parts the first time."

The next day I was asking the department heads whether we should hire this man. I asked the head of the economics department and he said, "Yes." The head of business education said, "Yes." The head of the management department, "Yes." I then asked Wilton Anderson, who had given the CPA exams for the whole United States for several years, if we should hire him. Wilton said, "I wouldn't touch him with a ten-foot pole." I said, "Why not?" And he replied, "Because he's a liar."

I said, "Wilton, that's a pretty serious accusation." And he said, "There is no way he could have taken the CPA exam in Ohio without having residency in that state."

So, I called the State of Ohio, and I asked them, "Could you please look up this man's record? See if he took the CPA exam." They couldn't find any record that he had taken it. I then called the man and said, "Look, we really don't care whether you're a CPA or not. You have a Ph.D. The only thing that's important is you said before a whole group of people that you had passed the CPA exam on the first try, and that's become an issue now. Will you please send us evidence that you passed the CPA exam." He said, "I'll send it right now."

About four days went by, and he finally called me. He said, "Please withdraw my name from consideration." Do you know, this man had never taken the CPA exam! I called his dean and told him what had happened. He said, "Well, you found out his weakness, didn't you? He just simply cannot resist enriching a good story. Whatever it is, he is likely to make it better."

Now here's a man who has every kind of talent in the world going for him, including physical appearance, mentality, everything except trustworthiness. You simply could not believe what he said.

Key #38

~ Understand the Importance ~ of Your Family

Your family can be very important to your success. Not only can it be a problem if you get a divorce, but a good wife or a good husband can be a terrific asset. Your spouse can be extremely important in your career. It is important to most men what goes on in their home and with their children. Knowing that they have a good wife at home and a woman who's taking care of their children can be a great blessing for a man.

My wife, Aasalee, has been my greatest asset and my children and grandchildren my greatest blessings.

As I said earlier, you will never make a more important decision than the person you marry. And so consequently, do a lot of thinking about that. I used to give a many commencement addresses, and I would always tell the young men, "Be sure and look at this young girl's mother, because she's going to look a whole lot more like her mother in 20 years than she looks like herself now."

The plain truth of the matter is that, in many cases, you'd be well advised to look into the family and what kind of family life they have before you decide whether or not to marry this person. To some degree, you marry into a family.

Spend time with your wife (or husband) and with your children. Time passes swiftly and before long your children will be gone from home.

If I can be personal for a moment, my wife, Aasalee, and I will celebrate our 55th anniversary September 19. She has been a great blessing to me, and deserves much of the credit for what success I have had. We have always been a team and she has always been supportive of my best efforts. There is no question that she has contributed greatly to our family. Our three daughters and our five grandchildren are the light of our lives and give meaning and purpose to our endeavors.

I was lying on my back in the hospital recently, and I realized that God, family, friends and my reputation were all that were important to me. As the story goes, a rich man died and they asked, "How much did he leave?" The answer, "All of it."

∞∞∞∞∞∞∞∞

H*er children arise up, and call her blessed; her husband also, and he praiseth her.*
> ~ *The Bible, Proverbs 31:28*

A *happy family is but an earlier heaven.*
> ~ *Bowring*

∞∞∞∞∞∞∞∞

The following two pages are my greatest lifelong blessings ... my family.

My wife, Aasalee, early in our marriage with our first-born daughter, Linda.

Dr. Eugene L. Swearingen

Eugene and Aasalee Swearingen and two younger daughters, Sherry, left, and Sandra, right.

Key #39

~ Manage Your Own Money ~

Your credit rating is something that is very important. For you women, it is important that you develop a credit rating of your own. You would be surprised how many women I have talked to, soon after a divorce, who suddenly found they had no credit. They had never bothered to establish any credit **in their own name**.

Buy insurance against major risks. I tell young people to buy term life insurance; **enough** is at least three times their annual income. Your family ought to be able to live for a period of time after your death without major financial problems. Usually young people cannot afford 20-year pay for life insurance. Now if you're an insurance agent, you may say, "Well, at some stage in their life they really ought to buy the other," and that's probably true.

You ought to have a savings program. Every young person today, I think, ought to be paying into an IRA. The government has never given us anything which is as favorable as the rules under which you can put away money into an IRA. Not only can you deduct that money for income tax purposes now, but you can accumulate earnings on that money until you're $70\,1/2$ years old (if you want to leave it that long) without paying any taxes on it until it is withdrawn. Any young couple today can become millionaires by the time they're 65 if they want to. All they have to do is always put the maximum that they can in an IRA. Then invest the funds wisely. (Note: The tax reform bill has reduced the attractiveness of the I.R.A., but the earnings still accumulate tax free until received by the taxpayer.)

It's amazing what compound interest does. John D. Rockefeller was once asked, "How did you make so much money?" He replied, "I was fortunate early in life to discover the principal of compound interest."

There are two things a Christian should do: Pay your church and pay yourself before you pay anybody else. By paying yourself, I mean, that regardless of what your income is, you ought to be saving something. You should be investing that money. If you use good sense in investing it, it's fantastic what it will amount to in a few years if you don't go in there and touch it.

We have many mutual funds now that you can put money into and make 10% or better compounded annually. Value Line is one of the better-known ones. If you had put $10,000 in 8 years ago, you would have more than doubled your money by now. That is true in three or four of their funds, not just one.

Home ownership. Almost every young couple should aspire to home ownership because again the government gives you a real tax advantage by letting you deduct the interest. Most of what you will be paying for your home in the early years will be interest. Therefore, having that as a deductible item becomes an extremely important benefit.

Spend your money on your highest priorities. Do not

yield to impulse buying. If you cannot control yourself, then don't use credit cards. If you cannot control yourself, have a bonfire and throw all of your credit cards into it! There are people who seemingly cannot resist spending on credit. But it all has to be paid back **with interest.** It is extremely important to use your money wisely.

Learn how to budget. Build a budget. Live by the budget! At the end of the month, you ought to be able to tell where your money went. A lot of people just can't.

Women should learn something about their husband's business. Let me ask you some questions: How many checking accounts does your husband have? As a banker, I can tell you that some men have checking accounts that the wife doesn't know anything about. There are a lot of women who don't even have the slightest idea how much money is in their husband's checking accounts. There are some women who do not know how many safety deposit boxes their husbands have or where they keeps their keys! There are some women who do not have a key to the office where their husband works.

I have a four-page list of things women ought to know about the family financial affairs. Where are the insurance policies? Who is the beneficiary? Is it being kept up-to-date? Who's paying the premiums? How much money are we talking about? All of these things women ought to know. Some women do really know about the business affairs of their family; but many do not. There are some families where the man just handles all of the business affairs, and the woman is left totally unprepared to manage an estate when the husband dies. We saw this time and time again at the bank.

Do you know Senator Robert Kerr of Oklahoma died without a will? He must have had more legal advice available to him than about any man in Oklahoma; yet he died without a will. Many people do not have their will brought up-to-date. If you have not revised your will in the last ten years, you should do so. Many people even have the wrong beneficiaries written down in their will. Times can change. There are some people who have been really surprised when the will was read!

∞∞∞∞∞∞∞∞∞

Be thou diligent to know the state of thy flocks, and look well to thy herds. For riches are not forever: and doth the crown endure to every generation?

~ *The Bible, Proverbs 27:23,24*

Take care of the pennies and the pounds will take care of themselves.

~ *Old Proverb*

Key #40

~ Keep Your Priorities ~ In Balance

What are your priorities? There are some kinds of competition which are beneficial. But there are other kinds which are just disastrous for people. Which types of competitions fit your priorities? Competing against your own previous performance can be a wonderful way of growing into a better person. But competing in spending against your "friend" may be ill-advised.

A good definition of **status** is buying something you don't need with money you don't have to impress people you don't like. "Keeping up with the Joneses" is a wasteful form of competition.

Winning is important, but winning with integrity is even more important. A number of the so-called self-help books make a basic mistake. It is not enough to look out for "number one." Ethics are important, and **how** you win may be more important than winning.

When we compete in order to become a better person, we are becoming more of what God intended. Wasting your potential is a sin. No sensible person wants to look back on his life and see wasted talent and ability. It is what we do, compared to that we could have done, that is important.

If we believe that we were created in the image of God, then we were not created to fail. God surely created us for success and happiness. Otherwise, why would we be given great potential? But we also were given the freedom of choice, and some of us make very bad choices. Good choices lead to a wonderful life – bad choices lead to our undoing.

Most of us were taught as children that "competition is good for us." If we can outrun another child **we win**. Our parents praise us for each victory. A good report card means happy parents. We learn to try to **beat others** when we should be trying to do our best. Competition with others places our life in the hands of others. In order to fulfill our potential, we must put aside competition **with others**. It is not dominance we seek, but freedom, self-assurance, self-initiative, lack of fear and self-reliance.

∞∞∞∞∞∞∞∞∞

I have learned, in whatsoever state I am, therewith to be content.
~ The Bible, Philippians 4:11

It is the contest that delights us, not the victory.

~ *Pascal*

Key #41

~ Demonstrate Courage ~

Winners are people who have learned not to "pass the buck." President Harry Truman gained fame by saying, "The buck stops here." Harry Truman accepted responsibility. He had to make the terrible decision to use the atomic bomb.

Do you have the courage to stick to your opinion? Can you say, "**No!**" when faced by pressure from your peers? Many young people are into drugs because they lacked the courage to say, "No!"

Do you have the courage to come back and try again after failure? God expects us to learn to fail successfully. Every life has failures and we have to learn to deal with them courageously. Lacking courage we may be afraid to try. We limit our growth because we do not have the faith to fail. We **aim** low so we can succeed. We fear that failure is final, but every child that learns to walk does so because he or she gets up after every fall and tries again.

To see what should be done, and not do it, displays a lack of courage. To know what should be said, and not say it, shows weakness of character. We need courage tempered by prudence and sensitivity for others.

Winston Churchill led Britain with courage and vision. He was able to inspire valor through his great ability to communicate.

Confucius said, "To see what is right, and not do it, is want of courage." Andrew Jackson said, "One man with courage makes a majority." So have courage, aim high, and go for the gold – **your very best!**

∞∞∞∞∞∞∞∞

T*rue courage is the firm resolve of virtue and reason.*
~ *Whitehead*

B*e strong and of good courage, and do it; fear not, nor be dismayed.*
~ *The Bible, I Chronicles 28:20*

A *great deal of talent is lost in this world for the want of a little courage.*
~ *Sydney Smith*

KEY #42

~ LEARN TO SPEAK EFFECTIVELY ~

For anybody who has any hesitancy about getting up before a group of people, I recommend joining Toastmasters Club. If you don't do that, then take every opportunity that you can to get up in front of people and express yourself. Get involved in volunteer work or Sunday School or whatever pleases you, so that you can get up in front of people with confidence and be at ease. There are some people, when they get in front of a group, whose minds become disassociated with their bodies. Their tongues will not work. They literally are terrified when this happens. I heard a woman say, "I was so shy I couldn't even lead in silent prayer."

I don't mean that you have to be a dynamic speaker and one that can really hold an audience. But everybody ought to be able to get up on their feet and express themselves fluently and effectively. It doesn't do any good to have good ideas if no one will buy them. I hear people say, "Oh, I'm no good at sales." Well, let me tell you, we are constantly selling ourselves. We are selling ourselves every time we apply for a job, every time we go in and meet new people. We are constantly in the sales business, even though we think we're not in the sales business. When I was president of Tulsa University, what

Dr. Eugene L. Swearingen

did I sell? I sold Tulsa University. Consequently, we are all in the sales business.

I've heard Oral Roberts say when somebody's complaining about the weather, "Look, I'm in sales, not management." He is obviously in sales. You don't run a big university and an international religious mission without being in sales. Somebody has to be sold. And I mean a lot of people with a lot of money.

Helpful hints then about getting up before a group: I have already urged you to get into Toastmasters or something where you will be forced to get up and express your ideas. It's best to know your subject before you get up to present it. If you know your subject well, this will help a great deal. Never read a prepared speech! Never, even though you've written it out before. Make some notes and talk from the notes. I have never heard anybody who's good enough at reading to hold an audience when they get up and read a speech.

Use body movements and gestures, and be aware of what you're doing. One of the things that I have noticed that many men will do, is they get their hand in their pocket and rattle the keys and money. It drives you crazy after about five minutes. You would think they could hear it, and do something about it. They are nervous, and they are not even aware of the fact that they are creating a real distraction from their speech.

Learn to project your voice. A lot of people, particularly women, have trouble projecting their voice. Get used to using a mike, and project your voice. Maintain eye contact with certain people in the audience. Do not try to look at everybody at once. But find somebody on each side of the room that you're going to look at. Find somebody in the middle that you're going to look at. Talk to them. When they indicate some sign of life, then you can go on to the next point. You can tell whether you're getting across by eye contact with people in the audience. Do not look at an audience as one "group" of people. You're talking to a whole bunch of individuals, and you're having to communicate with everyone of these people as an individual, not as a group of people.

Eye contact is very important. Just keep speaking. I have seen people who took over a job such as Miss America. It's amazing the difference between a Miss America the day she becomes Miss America and a year later when she's turning it over to somebody else. The exposure that she's had, the number of times that she had to get up in front of a group and express herself, results in a tremendous amount of growth in that period of time. People in all other jobs where they are constantly having to express themselves become better and better at speaking.

> A *word fitly spoken is like apples of gold in pictures of silver.*
> ~ *The Bible, Proverbs 25:11*

KEY #43

~ Use Good Manners ~

Use good manners. Be courteous. Be polite. **Think of other people**. For those who are smokers, I would say particularly, think of other people. I quit smoking when I was 12 years old, so I have no sympathy for people who smoke. People are becoming more and more concerned about smoke and about the fact that it involves other people.

Courtesy is contagious. Nothing costs so little and goes so far. Courtesy will unlock doors, create friendships, build good will, inspire respect, and please those whose business it is to judge your performance.

Politeness costs nothing but pays big dividends. Kindness can become a habit, just as cruelty can. The choice is yours! And the choices you make will determine the kind of person you become.

Recruiters often take a prospective employee to dinner to observe his or her table manners. Would you pass the test?

Emily Post says, "No one....can fail to gain from a proper, courteous, likeable approach, or fail to be handicapped by an improper, offensive, resentful one."

Etiquette to me is not a set of rules. Rather it is a matter of good taste, of concern for others, and faithfulness to loyalty, integrity, and love, for ourselves and our fellow man.

∞∞∞∞∞∞∞∞

Good manners are stronger than laws.
~ *Carlile*

There is no policy like politeness; and good manners are the best thing in the world to get a good name.
~ *Bulwer*

Let your speech be always with grace....
~ *The Bible, Colossians 4:6*

All doors open to courtesy.
~ *Thomas Fuller*

KEY #44

~ BECOME A GOOD COMMUNICATOR ~

In order to do this, we must recognize the process that goes on in communication. First of all, we usually try to communicate by words. And words have no meaning except the meaning which we attach to them. Therefore, if I am communicating with you, I must first assume something about your vocabulary. If you speak only French, you see, I've got a problem. On the other hand, I might assume that you speak English, and hopefully you do.

To communicate something to you, I start with an abstraction in my mind. That abstraction has to be coded. By coding it, I mean I have to put it into words. In order to code it, I will choose from my vocabulary hopefully those words which you will understand.

Dan Divine, when he was coach at Missouri, told about how the game was not going well, and he grabbed this great big tackle off the bench and he said, "Go in there and get rambunctious." Well, the tackle starts onto the field and then comes back and says, "What's his number, coach?"

You see, if the word 'rambunctious' is not in his vocabulary, then he attaches whatever meaning seems appropriate. And for him, "get rambunctious" meant somebody was out there he was supposed to **get**. You have to use words that are not only in your vocabulary, but are also in the other person's vocabulary.

When you are going to communicate, you must choose the time and place and whether it's going to be a face-to-face verbal communication or a telephone call. We like face-to-face communication because we can read the person's eyes and expressions. I have seen a person fly to Chicago, and another person fly from New York to Chicago to meet for one hour just so they can be face-to-face and talk. That is a good indication that face-to-face communication is an extremely important thing. Because we are less likely to read the wrong symbols, we're less likely to arrive at the wrong conclusion about what is meant by this particular conversation. I don't know many businessmen who will conclude a major deal without it being face-to-face. It's very important to have that kind of communication.

Now, another thing about communication – I believe we have to be very careful that we are not prejudging other people or thinking about them in a certain way. I will tell you one story which I think illustrates this. This is the story of two people who were sitting on a park bench. One was an Oriental and the other was Jewish. The Jewish man hauls off and knocks the Oriental man off the bench. He gets up, dusts himself off, and says, "Well, what in the world was that for?" The Jew replied, "That was for Pearl Harbor," to which the Oriental replied, "But I'm Chinese. I'm not Japanese." The Jew says, "Oh, you're yellow; you all look alike to me." So they sat there a while longer and it wasn't long before the Oriental hauled off and knocked the Jewish man off the bench. The Jew gets up, dusts himself off, and says, "Well, what in the world was that for?" The Oriental replied, "That's for the Titanic." The Jew thought a minute and said, "The Titanic! That was sunk by an iceberg!" The Oriental replied, "Well, Iceberg, Goldberg, Greenberg; you're all alike to me!"

I trust you will not see this as an ethnic joke, of which I do not approve. This story merely illustrates that words can have different meanings to different people. Communication is extremely important.

When I was a Boy Scout Executive at Texarkana, Arkansas-Texas, we had a secretary who was not very bright. My boss came home from camp one summer and the secretary said to him, "We're out of Cub Scout application forms." He said, "My Lord, with school starting, we're going to need a million of them!" And she said, "Well, what should I do?" He said, "Order them." So she sat down and ordered **one million** Cub Scout forms.

The firm that got this order knew that there were only two million Cub Scouts in the whole United States. So they sent a telegram back and said, "We have your order for one million Cub Scout application forms. We think this must be an error. Will you please confirm the order?" My boss came back from Scout camp and the secretary said, "They want confirmation on that order of Cub Scout application forms." He said, "Well, confirm it!" She sat down and confirmed the order.

In September, they drove up in front of City Hall where the Scout offices were located with one million Cub Scout application forms. My boss immediately fired the secretary. Then they had an emergency board meeting. They then fired the Scout Executive. That was in 1943, and it was 1946 before they had enough money collected to pay off the bill for one million Cub Scout application forms.

I used to think that was the most horrible incident I'd ever heard of, but I'm going to give you another illustration of miscommunication that is just about as extreme. One Monday morning at the bank I got a call from the Investment Division. The Caller said, "Are you going to be in the office for a little while?" I said, "Yes." He said, "We have a real problem. We want to come over." So they came over, and I finally got this story out of them.

On Friday afternoon, a man had come in about 2:00 p.m. wanting to sell a $500 Sinclair mini-bond. This bond was issued during the depression of the 1930's and, contrary to most bonds, was in $500 denominations instead of $1,000's, so he had a very unique $500 bond. We were going to get it "cashed" for him, and the charge on that would have been $10. That's all we would have made on that transaction.

The man who normally sold the bonds turned to a girl who had only sold treasury bills (although she'd been in the bank two years) and said, "Here, get some experience in selling a bond." Well, she wanted to be very professional so she called up a broker at Dean Witter and said, "I have a 500 Sinclair convertible to go." The broker said, "Well, I'm going to have to call New York on this." And she said, "Fine, call New York." Shortly, he called back and gave her a quote. She said, "Sold." That was on Friday afternoon.

On Monday morning, we got a confirmation that we

had sold a $500,000 Sinclair bond. The girl immediately called the broker and said it wasn't a $500,000 bond, but it was a $500 bond. He said, "For heaven's sake, don't tell anybody. We're going to have to cover with Atlantic Richfield stock." (Sinclair had sold to Atlantic Richfield.) They said, "If anybody finds out we're short that much stock, we're in trouble. So don't say a thing. We'll start buying a little bit at every Dean Witter office around the country."

They began to buy and gradually the price went up, up, up and at the end of the week, we had filled the order. On Friday, we totaled up our losses and we had lost $98,000 on a transaction which at most would have given us a $10 profit. So then the question was, "Whose fault is it?" Dean Witter said, "500 to go means in the trade $500,000." Our bond people had to agree that that's what it meant. The girl who sold the bond was crying and was saying, "But I didn't say $500,000. I said 500 to go."

We finally agreed that Dean Witter should have confirmed the order with us. We decided that we were both at error. We split the loss $49,000 to each of us. Then the question was, "What are we going to do with the girl?" Shall we fire her or not? The man who handed her the bond said, "Look, I'm the bond man. If I was going to give her the responsibility, I should have trained her. I should have done a follow-up to make sure she had done it properly. I gave her the job to do, and I hadn't trained her. So, if anybody's going to be fired, it ought to be me." I agreed, but I didn't fire him.

I will always remember how easy it is to fowl up a communication, because words have no meaning except the meaning which we attach to them. And people do have different meanings for the same words.

It is extremely important as you move up in management that you spend more and more time listening and less and less time talking. As you move up in an organization, you have less first-hand information about what's going on in your organization. You're going to have to get more and more information from other people. This information comes to you on the telephone, it comes in conversations, it comes in reports. There is no more important skill that you can have as a manager than to be a good listener. Good listeners attract other people. People like them. They have a certain something – we call it charisma. There's a certain personal magnetism about good listeners. People like to talk to them. Listening is a skill that can be learned, and you need to learn it.

Listening requires a certain type of attitude. Unless you have it, you will not be a good listener. To be a good listener, eye contact is extremely important. In the Bible we have several statements about Jesus' eyes. His eyes apparently were magnetic. People were entranced as they looked at Him and as He looked at them. Consequently, being able to look deeply into other people's souls and make them feel important is a vital part of listening. God gave us two ears and only one mouth. He knew it was more important to listen than to talk. Use eye language. It is important that you be able to smile with your eyes. It is almost impossible to smile with your lips until you begin to smile first with your eyes. When your eyes begin to smile you see the corner of your eyes begin to change and then you can smile. The tone of your voice, the way you ask questions – all of these are important tools in listening.

Dr. Eugene L. Swearingen

Key #45

~ Develop Your Human ~ Relations Skills

I tell young people that their success will be determined more by their ability to deal with human relation problems than it will by skills in a particular area such as accounting or engineering. The further you go in your profession, the more important your human relations skills become, and the less important are those technical skills.

The Bible has a pretty good prescription for human relations. Treat other people exactly as you would like for them to treat you. There are some people in organizations that are what we call **people growers**. People blossom under them. There are other people who simply destroy the people around them, particularly the people under them.

One of the things that is expected of all people in a corporation is self-control. If you are not able to control yourself, you're going to find the corporate world a very difficult place in which to work. When you go into a corporation, people do not expect you to display your anger, but rather to be able to control yourself. The higher you go in an organization, the less you'll be excused for losing control of your own behavior. In other words, maybe down at the bottom of an organization you can lose control once in a while and get by with it, but as you move up in that organization, you are expected to have yourself under complete control.

Treating confidential material confidentially is extremely important. I know of a bank director who was asked to leave a Board of Directors because his wife was finding out within an hour after he came home from a board meeting what went on at that meeting. Within two hours, the people at the country club knew what had happened. Since he could not refrain from telling her, and she obviously couldn't keep her mouth shut about what he was telling her, the bank had to request this man's resignation from the board. He was a powerful man, but they simply could not afford those kind of leaks.

∞∞∞∞∞∞∞∞∞∞

>Prudence is a quality incompatible with vice, and can never be effectively enlisted in its cause.
>
>~ Burke

>A tailbearer revealeth secrets: but he that is of a faithful spirit concealeth the matter.
>
>~ The Bible, Proverbs 11:13

Key #46

~ Become a Problem Solver ~

For some ten years, I was a labor arbitrator, and I learned what I knew about labor arbitration from a man at Oklahoma State University by the name of Ed Burris. Ed told me that the first thing you should do when you sit down to arbitrate a dispute is to get **in writing** what the problem is that they want you to arbitrate. He said, "Let me tell you what happened to me."

Ed went from Stillwater, Oklahoma, down to Galveston, Texas, to arbitrate a labor dispute. Labor always sits on one side of the table. Management representatives sit on the other side of the table. The arbitrator sits at the head of the table in a neutral position. Ed asked management what the problem was that he was to arbitrate. Management stated the problem, and the labor union said, "No, that isn't what we want arbitrated." Ed said, "Well, then you state the problem." The union tried to state the problem, and management said, "No," they didn't agree. Finally, Ed Burris said, "Look, I'm going down to the lounge at the end of the hall. You all decide what it is you want me to arbitrate. I'll come back when you're ready."

They came to get him in about an hour. With a sheepish look on their faces they said, "Send us your bill. We don't have a problem." Can you image that – through all the steps in labor arbitration up to the final act of calling in an arbitrator, they had never really agreed on what it was they were arguing about!

When you're talking about a problem, the first thing to do is to **define what the problem is**. Sometimes you will find that the problem is more than one problem and can be broken down into several different problems, and you can attack them separately rather than all at one time. In many cases, what looks like the problem is nothing more than an effect caused by some other problem. So you need to find out whether or not this is the basic problem or a symptom of the problem.

Define the problem. Break it down into separate problems if you can. Then gather all of the facts and opinions you can get together. Once you've gone through this process, define what your alternatives are. You don't need to worry about things you can't do anything about. So consequently, find out what alternatives you have. If the problem is the boss' son, and you don't like the way he's running the company, forget it – he's the son, and there's nothing you can do about it. You just have to accept the situation – or get out of the firm if you don't like it.

In any case, define what your alternatives are. List the pros and cons of each alternative. What do you think are the good and bad points of doing it each way? Then, finally, evaluate those pros and cons and choose your best alternative. Next, implement your decision. Finally, get feedback as to how it's working. And if it isn't working right, then begin the process again. That's right,

Start over.

I'm convinced that with the above set of steps you can deal with any kind of problem. You can deal with family problems. You can deal with business problems – any kind of problems you may have.

∞∞∞∞∞∞∞∞

It is useless to attempt to reason a man out of a thing he was never reasoned into.
> ~ *Swift*

He that answereth a matter before he heareth it, it is folly and shame unto him.
> ~ *The Bible, Proverbs 18:13*

Reason is our intellectual eye, and like the bodily eye it needs light to see; and to see clearly and far, it needs the light of heaven.
> ~ *Shakespeare*

KEY #47

~ Know How to Give a ~ 60-Second Praise

I want to recommend some reading for you. There are three books that I regard as the three top books that should be on the businessman's shelf today. One of them is, *In Search of Excellence,* which describes why certain corporations are regarded as excellently managed and others are not.

The second book is *Megatrends* by John Naisbitt, which gives you a very good idea of what is going to happen in our society through the next 20-30 years, into the next century. And finally, a little book which is very thin, but I think very good, entitled *The One-Minute Manager* by Kenneth Blanchard and Spencer Johnson. This book also has a couple of tapes to go with it. So, if you've read the book, you may want to get the tapes.

The One-Minute Manager asks, "Can you give a one-minute praising?" We have an excellent film that we use in a class on job appraisal. Appraising how a person is doing on their job, or "performance appraisal" as it is called. Most people in corporations do not like to do performance appraisals. And the reason they don't, is because there was never an agreed upon **set of goals** between the boss and the subordinate. If there were some goals that were measurable, and they had agreed upon what should be done then they wouldn't mind measuring.

It's important to clearly define quantitative goals. But if they have never agreed upon any set of goals, then obviously what they do is get down to saying, "Well, I don't like the way you wear your tie." He says, "I don't care. It doesn't make any difference whether I wear a tie or not. I perform." You know what we should be doing in a performance appraisal? We ought to be measuring their performance, shouldn't we? Instead, quite often what we measure is whether we like them, whether they've got a good personality, whether they dress the way we think they should dress, or whether they wear their hair the way we think they ought to wear it. We never get around to asking the fundamental question: "How much did this guy sell last year?" (Or whatever measures results)

Many times as bosses, we measure how many calls the employee made, not how many sales he made. It doesn't make any difference how many calls he made if he didn't make any sales! Sometimes we're measuring the wrong thing. **The workers respect what the boss respects**.

Now if you're going to give a one-minute praising, these two authors, Kenneth Blanchard and Spencer Johnson, say there are several things that you ought to do. One is tell people up front that you're going to let them know how they're doing. "I'm going to tell you whether you're performing well or whether you're not performing well. Particularly if you're not performing well. I'm not going to wait until next quarter when the performance review comes around. I'm going to tell you when anything bad happens, that you should not have done that. Your performance can be improved." Tell people up front that their performance is going to be measured.

Another point, when you want to praise people, do it now. Don't put it off until some later date. If people deserve praise, give it to them now! Incidentally, suppose you have two secretaries. One has been with you ten years and the other for two weeks. Which one are you most likely to tell they've done a good job? The one who's been here two weeks! You say, "My other secretary; I told her last year she was doing a good job." And that's the way we are sometimes. That's about how often we praise our people. The people that you are most likely not to tell that you appreciate them are your friends, your closest family members, and the employees who work for you. And those are the very people you should be telling how much you do appreciate them. They are the ones who are closest to you and mean the most to you.

Third point, tell people what they did right. Be specific. Tell them exactly what they did right. Tell people how good you feel about the fact that what they're doing is right. Blanchard and Johnson say, "After you tell them how good they've done, stop for a moment and let them feel how good you feel about the fact that they have done a good job. Encourage them to do more of the same. Tell them to keep on doing a good job." And then *The One Minute Manager* suggests, "Shake hands or touch them. Touch them to let them know that they are important to you and that their success is important to you."

This can all be done in a minute or two. That's all it takes. You don't have to have a formal performance review to tell people they've done a good job. We shouldn't wait for that. You ought to do it when they've done a good job.

∞∞∞∞∞∞∞∞∞∞

A ppreciative words are the most powerful force for good on earth!
~ George W. Crane

Whenever you commend, add your reasons for doing so.
~ Steele

KEY #48

~ KNOW HOW TO GIVE A ~
60-SECOND REPRIMAND

This also comes out of the book, *The One-Minute Manager*. These rules are given: "Tell people beforehand that you're going to let them know how they are doing, and you're going to do it candidly and in no uncertain terms. You are going to tell them how they are performing. You're going to evaluate their work." Reprimand people immediately when something goes wrong. Don't let it fester by waiting for a long time.

I have another rule and that is, **never reprimand an employee in front of other employees.** You may want to take the employee in your office and talk to him or her there. Tell the employee specifically what he or she did wrong. Stop for a few seconds of uncomfortable silence to let it sink in.

Finally, shake hands or touch the employee in some way. Put your hand on his shoulder or something, to let him know that you really are on his side even though he has done wrong. Remind him how much you value each employee. Be careful that you don't destroy the self-worth of a person. If you have employees and you reprimand them in such a way that they lose all faith, or they lose their self-confidence, or their self-image is severely damaged, then they won't be worth much to you.

So in reprimanding them say, "We're counting on you to do better." Reaffirm that you think well of them, but not of their performance. You see, there's a real difference between telling people that "they're no darn good" and saying, "Your performance is unsatisfactory." In fact, what you want is for people to feel that you think they are worth something even though their performance was not good.

Finally, when the reprimand is over, it's over. Forget it. You have already done it, now forget it and get on with your business.

∞∞∞∞∞∞∞∞

R*eprove thy friend privately; commend him or her publicly.*
~ Solon

H*e that regardeth reproof shall be honoured.*
~ The Bible, Proverbs 13:18

C*orrection does much, but encouragement does more.*
~ Goethe

KEY #49

~ BE ENTHUSIASTIC ! ~

I mentioned the book by Frank Betger, *How I Changed Myself From Failure To Success In Selling.* Somebody told me it's out of print, but I have a copy of it and I know that there must be a lot of libraries that still have copies of this book. If you can't find that one, there's another one written by Charlie Jones called *Life Is Tremendous.* The author is called "Tremendous Charlie Jones."

Zig Zigler is another one with enthusiasm just spilling over. Robert Schuller has this same type of excitement. You can learn a lot from listening to Zig Zigler's or Robert Schuller's tapes. There's a wonderful book that Schuller has written entitled *The Peak to Peek Principle.* Schuller says, "The way we climb mountains is like the way we go through life. We get up to the top of the first range of mountains and we've reached a peak. But when we reach that peak, then we get a peek (a glance) at the next range of mountains. When we crawl to the top of the highest one of those, we suddenly look over and we see another range of mountains behind that's even higher." He goes on to say, "That's the way we go through life. We set goals. We accomplish them. Then we see that there are even bigger and more challenging goals ahead." So we progress to greater things.

If you haven't read the book *Enthusiasm Makes the Difference*, by Norman Vincent Peale, I recommend that book to you also.

While I served on the board of Parker Drilling company for 25 years, I observed that Robert Parker, Sr. is one of the best speakers that I've ever heard in front of any group. Every time, the one quality that you absolutely feel, if you're in the audience, is his tremendous enthusiasm for life. You can just feel the vibrations coming from that man and it affects audiences. It affects them favorably. They give him standing ovations.

People do respond to people who are enthusiastic about life. And they respond also to people who are real dullards, but they respond in a different way. If you want an enthusiastic response, give an enthusiastic message.

∞∞∞∞∞∞∞∞

Every production of genius must be the production of enthusiasm.
~ *Disraeli*

Nothing is so contagious as enthusiasm. It is the genius of sincerity, and truth accomplishes no victories without it.
~ *Bulwer*

KEY #50

~ LEARN TO THINK BIG ~

Stanley Draper, who was the Secretary of the Chamber of Commerce in Oklahoma City, would call Dr. Bennett, President of Oklahoma State University, and say, "Dr. Bennett, come down to Oklahoma City. Let's get a conference room in a hotel and **think big**." And they would think big.

I understand the decision to build the first dormitory at Oklahoma State came out of one of these sessions. They agreed, "We've got to have the right to issue revenue bonds that the dormitory revenue can retire." This was during the depression of the 1930's. Stanley Draper said, "I'll get E. K. Gaylord to help me, and we will get Governor "Alfalfa Bill" Murray to allow us to pass this bond issue." Murray was promised that **if** he allowed them to pass this revenue bond issue, the first dormitory would be named for him.

Some of you have seen Murray Hall on the Oklahoma State University campus. When Governor Murray came up for the dedication, he wanted to be sure that they were not going to be able to change the name after he left the governor's chair. They said he got a ladder and crawled up to find out if the carving of "Murray Hall" was actually one inch deep. That's what he had required. It was going to be one inch deep in marble so that it could never be taken off. In being a big thinker, don't use excuses. Do become a dreamer. Get rid of your fears. Build confidence in yourself and the people around you. Learn to smile big. If you want people to believe that you are on fire and really going someplace, walk 25% faster. That sounds funny, but you try doing it; it will make you feel like a different person.

Have you ever gone to a large mall at 8:00 a.m.? You ought to go and watch some of those women who are 70-years-old walk. I have to dog-trot to keep up with some of those ladies. It's unbelievable how fast they can walk. But they've been walking every morning. There are hundreds of them. I can't imagine anything better for a lot of people than to get out and walk. Some of them walk five miles a day. Walk 25% faster.

Don't sell yourself short. Stretch your vision. What is your magnificent obsession. The Bible says, "People without a vision will perish." Get the big view of your life and don't worry about trivial things. God has said, "All things are possible to him that believeth." So start believing big dreams. Get yourself prepared to accomplish things that you had never thought possible before. People do it all the time. But first, it has to begin up in this little box that we call our mind. It is so important that we have faith, and that we also have a belief in ourselves. Robert Louis Stevenson said, "To be what we are and to become what we're capable of becoming is the only end of life."

These **50 KEYS** will change your life for the better if you let them. It is your choice! Use them to unlock the doors leading to your **SUCCESS AND BEYOND!**

Your Personal Key Notes Applied from Success and Beyond

Your Personal Key Notes Applied from Success and Beyond

Your Personal Key Notes Applied from Success and Beyond

Your Personal Key Notes Applied from Success and Beyond

Final Key Comment

Goals

Open

A

Life to

Success

"I wish you the very best in all you do."
~ *Eugene Swearingen*